BRIGHT IDEAS FOR SEASONAL ACTIVITIES

from *Scholastic Magazines*

Ward Lock Educational/Scholastic

CONTENTS

Published by Scholastic Publications (Magazines) Ltd and Ward Lock Educational Co Ltd.

© 1984 Scholastic Publications (Magazines) Ltd

Ward Lock Educational Co Ltd
47 Marylebone Lane London W1A 6AX
A Ling Kee Company

Scholastic Publications (Magazines) Ltd
9 Parade Leamington Spa
Warwickshire CV32 4DG

Ideas drawn from Scholastic's magazines, including *Child Education, Junior Education* and *Art and Craft*.

Compiled by Janet Eyre with additional mathematical material from Julia Matthews
Edited by Sue Quilliam
Illustrated by Sue Lines

ISBN 0-7062-4453-2

Front cover: Horse-chestnut leaves. Oxford Scientific Films. Back cover: Virginia creeper, Oxford Scientific Films.

INTRODUCTION

Seasons come, seasons go, but the need for fresh seasonal ideas to use in the primary classroom remains constant. You will find many ideas in this book, covering the activities, natural phenomena and special days associated with each season. There are some for each curriculum area – maths, science, language, cookery, music, movement, craft – and many which fall into several categories. All the material has been tried and tested and is drawn from Scholastic magazines. There is also some additional mathematical material which has been specially written for the book.

The seasonal ideas given are aimed at helping children to observe and experience the world around them at different times of the year. Cultural festivals are not included as this would be a whole, separate book. We plan to publish a *Bright Ideas* book on festivals later in this series. Christmas is covered in more detail in *Bright Ideas for Christmas Art and Craft*, already published in this series.

HOW TO USE THE BOOK

The book is divided into four sections, each covering a different season. At the beginning of each section you will find two lists, one of things to collect and display, and the other of topics associated with the season. The lists are designed to help you plan your topic work; within each section you will find related ideas to get you started.

The following information is given for each idea:

Age range – an appropriate age range is suggested, but this is intended to be a rough guide only. You may find that an idea for nine- to eleven-year-olds could be adapted for younger children, and vice versa.

Group size – the group sizes given (individuals, small group, large group or whole class) are intended to help you organize the activities. Once again, you should regard these as flexible; you may want to adapt them to suit your own situation and teaching style.

What you need – a list of all the materials you will need to carry out the activity. Most of these will be readily available in the average classroom; if not, they can be obtained easily. Be sure to have all the materials to hand before embarking on the activity.

What to do – how to carry out the activity.

Follow-up – suggestions for follow-up work are given, where appropriate, to help you extend the activity and explore possible avenues of interest.

Dip into the book, find something to use as a quick filler, or link several ideas to form the basis of a topic and help your children become more aware of the changing seasons as well as the significance of seasonal events.

Janet Eyre

SPRING

Displays and collections

Eggs
Egg-cups
Egg-timers
Spring flowers
Old nests (baked in the oven to kill insects)
Prisms (rainbows)
Cleaning tools: brushes, mops, dusters, buckets, etc
Yellow and green things
Weather-vanes
Kites
Little things

Topic work

Nest building
Young animals
Wind
Flight
Air
Growth
Families
Dragons
The spectrum and light
Colours
Customs
Weather
Spring-cleaning
Frogs
Spring flowers and blossoms
Eggs
Birds returning from warmer countries

The first day of spring

Age range
Seven to nine.

Group size
Whole class.

What to do
The first day of spring is 21 March. Encourage the children to talk about spring; what it means to them; what associations it has.

From a daily newspaper, find out the times of sunrise and sunset on 21 March, then work out how many hours of daylight and darkness there are. Shine a torch, projector or Anglepoise light on a globe to demonstrate night and day. Which is longer, day or night?

Follow-up
Discuss the change to British Summer Time. Ask the children to write about it – what will they do in the extra hour of daylight at the end of the day?

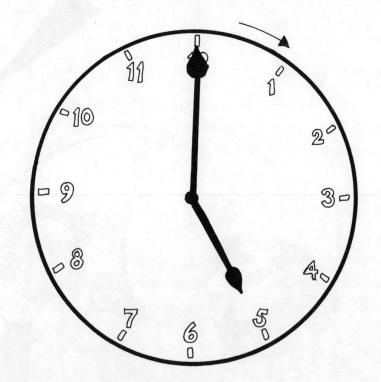

A weather saying to check

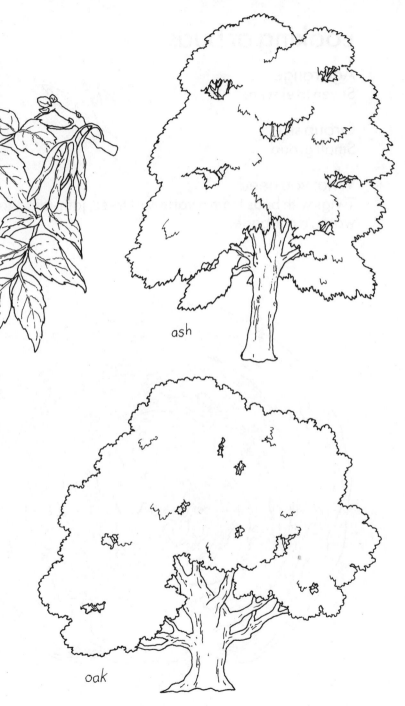

Age range
Seven to nine.

Group size
Whole class.

What to do
Find an oak and an ash tree somewhere near school. Look at the trees once a day for two or three weeks in spring and notice when the buds break into leaf. Write down the date for each tree. Make a record of the weather which follows these dates, then decide whether, this year, the following old saying about the weather is true:

'Ash before oak, we'll have a soak (heavy rain),
Oak before ash, we'll have a splash (light rain).'

Follow-up
Ask the children if they can think of other old weather sayings. Get them to ask adults if they know any. Make a poster of sayings and illustrate them.

ash

oak

Looking at buds

Age range
Seven to eleven.

Group size
Small group.

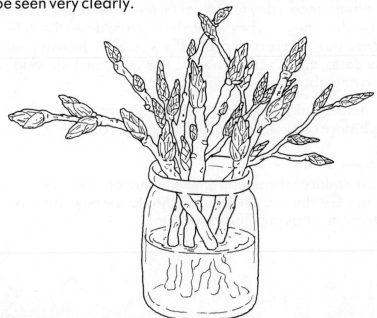

What you need
Twigs with buds from a variety of trees, jam-jars, warm water, a cabbage.

What to do
If possible, take the children out to collect buds; take only one twig from each tree. Back in the classroom, put the twigs in water in a warm place and watch the buds unfold. Do they all unfold in the same way?

Let the children take one unopened bud each and carefully peel away the sections, working slowly into the centre. As they work, they should lay the parts out on a piece of paper in the order in which they remove them. Compare the pieces from different buds.

Gather the children together, then cut a cabbage in half. A cabbage is one of the largest buds, so its structure can be seen very clearly.

Follow-up
Make observational drawings of the buds as they unfold and of the structure of the buds examined. Encourage the children to draw in great detail – the results can be beautiful.

Label the drawings with appropriate vocabulary.

Leafy silhouettes

Age range
Seven to eleven.

Group size
Whole class.

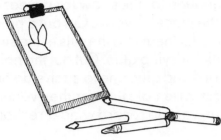

What you need
Clipboards, paper, pencils, pens, crayons or felt-tipped pens.

What to do
Take the children out armed with clipboards, paper, pencils, pens and crayons, to look at trees. Go right underneath the trees and look upwards, through the branches and leaves. Look closely to see the variations in the colours of leaves, the position of the leaves on the branches, the pattern of the branches themselves and how they overlap. Make observational drawings.

Follow-up
Back in the classroom, draw and cut out a series of leaves from paper and paste them lightly to a window. By overlapping some of the leaves, the dappled effect of light coming through branches can be reproduced.

Weather-vane

Age range
Seven to eleven.

Group size
Small group.

What you need
A plastic drinking straw, scissors, a pin, a piece of stick (square-sided if possible), card, glue, a compass.

What to do
Cut a slit 1cm long in each end of the straw. Push the pin through the exact centre of the straw, making the hole large enough for the straw to spin easily, and on into the top of the piece of wood. Cut out a pointer and tail from card and fix them into the slits in the straw. Secure them with quick-drying glue. Cut out the points of the compass from card and glue one to each side of the stick. Using the compass, orientate the weather-vane. Use the weather-vane to record wind direction.

Follow-up
Explain to the children what a westerly wind, northerly wind, etc, is. Make a wind rose to show the prevailing wind over a given period. The children can make a graph of their daily results.

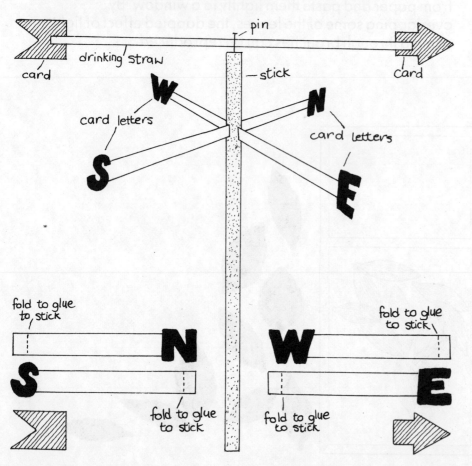

pin

drinking straw

card

stick

card

card letters

card letters

W

S

N

E

fold to glue to stick

fold to glue to stick

fold to glue to stick

fold to glue to stick

N

S

W

E

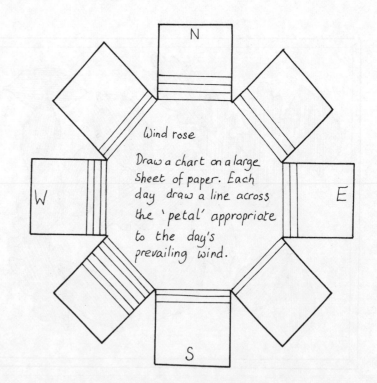

N

W

E

S

Wind rose

Draw a chart on a large sheet of paper. Each day draw a line across the 'petal' appropriate to the day's prevailing wind.

Mad March wind

Age range
Five to seven.

Mad March wind went out to play.
'I'll have such fun', said he, 'today.
I'll toss the clothes put out to dry
And chase the clouds across the sky.

'And when the boys and girls come out
I'll blow their scarves and hats about;
I'll tangle up their curly hair
And fling their kites high in the air'.

The mad March wind rushed up and down
And whirled through all the streets in town,
Until, at last, tired out with play
He turned and softly blew away.

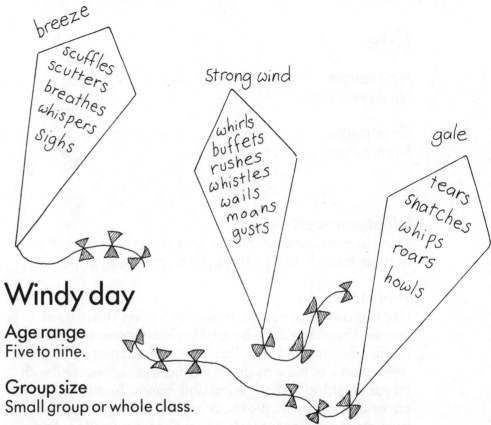

breeze
scuffles
scutters
breathes
whispers
sighs

strong wind
whirls
buffets
rushes
whistles
wails
moans
gusts

gale
tears
snatches
whips
roars
howls

Windy day

Age range
Five to nine.

Group size
Small group or whole class.

What to do
Go outside on a windy day. What can the children hear, see, smell and feel? Make a list of words to describe each of the following types of wind: a breeze, a strong wind, a gale.

Follow-up
Read some 'windy' poems (for example, 'The Wind and Windy Nights' by R L Stevenson), then use the word banks to help with writing some of your own.

Use percussion instruments to imitate the sound of each type of wind. Create a sound picture of a breeze gradually building up into a strong wind, then a gale, then dying down again.

Kite

Age range
Nine to eleven.

Group size
Small group.

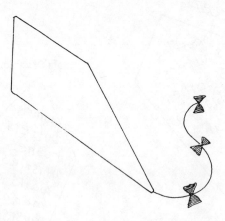

What you need
Cane (6 mm diameter) or bamboo canes split down the middle, thick thread or string, linen, plastic or paper.

What to do
Use two pieces of cane to make the frame. The ratio of lengths should be 3:2, so that if the longer piece is 60 cm, the shorter will be 40 cm. Position the crosspiece about one seventh of the way down the main stick. Secure it with thread or string lashed round both canes. Make the kite covering from linen, plastic or paper, sewing or stapling pockets at each corner into which the frame will fit. Add a tail – on a linen kite you will need a cloth tail of about 75 cm, while on a plastic one you will need a continuous length of plastic about 2 cm wide. Attach the kite string to the cross-section of the canes. **Do take care when working with split cane – it can be very sharp.**

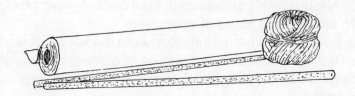

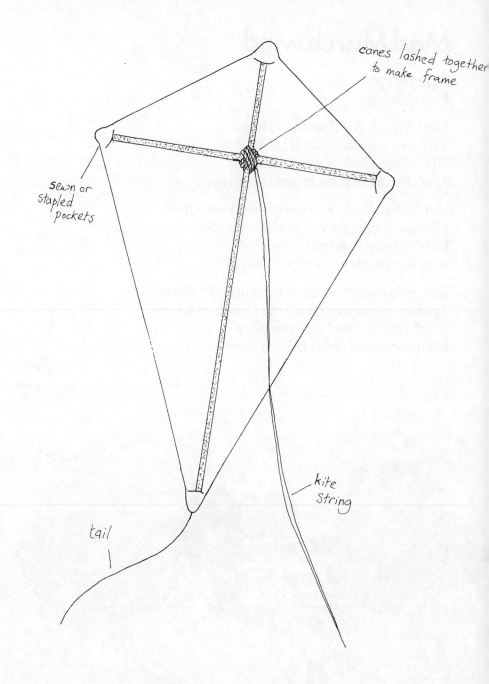

canes lashed together to make frame

sewn or stapled pockets

kite string

tail

Flyaway kite

Age range
Seven to eleven.

Group size
Individuals.

What to do
The children imagine being a kite which escapes from its owner on a windy day. Each writes a story about where he/she goes, what happens to him/her and how he/she gets back to his/her owner.

Follow-up
Display the stories on kite-shaped mounts.

Kite-flying

Age range
Nine to eleven.

Group size
Small group.

What you need
A kite (see page 14 for instructions), a spring balance, light string.

What to do
On a windy day, take the children out to test the kite. Measure the tug on the string, using a spring balance. Estimate how high the kite is flying, then check by means of a light string tied to the kite tail. Ask: 'What would happen if you let go of the string?' and 'Why does the kite need a tail?'

Follow-up
Let the children record their findings. Test the kite on other days to see how the tug on the string differs with different wind strengths.

Orange bread

Age range
Seven to nine.

Group size
Small group.

What you need
170 g flour
85 g sugar
rind and juice of 1 orange
1×15 ml spoon of marmalade
1×15 ml spoon of cooking oil
1 egg
a little milk
butter for greasing and spreading

What to do
Put the flour and sugar in a bowl. Add the grated rind of
the orange, together with the marmalade, oil and orange
juice. Beat the egg with a little milk and add it to the
mixture. Pour the mixture into a greased loaf tin and bake
for 40 minutes at 375°F/90°C or gas mark 5. When cool,
slice the bread and spread it with butter and marmalade.

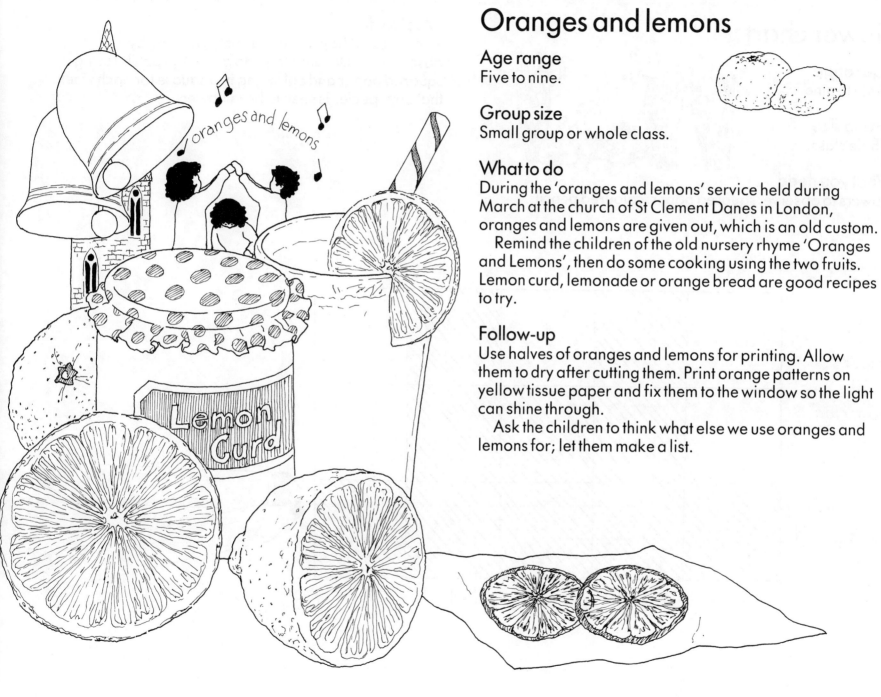

Oranges and lemons

Age range
Five to nine.

Group size
Small group or whole class.

What to do
During the 'oranges and lemons' service held during March at the church of St Clement Danes in London, oranges and lemons are given out, which is an old custom.

Remind the children of the old nursery rhyme 'Oranges and Lemons', then do some cooking using the two fruits. Lemon curd, lemonade or orange bread are good recipes to try.

Follow-up
Use halves of oranges and lemons for printing. Allow them to dry after cutting them. Print orange patterns on yellow tissue paper and fix them to the window so the light can shine through.

Ask the children to think what else we use oranges and lemons for; let them make a list.

Flower chart

Age range
Seven to nine.

Group size
Whole class.

What you need
Flowers to observe, squared paper, coloured pencils.

What to do
Make a list of flowers in order of flowering by observation. Develop this into a block graph by using squared paper and colouring in a square for each week that any species is seen to be in flower.

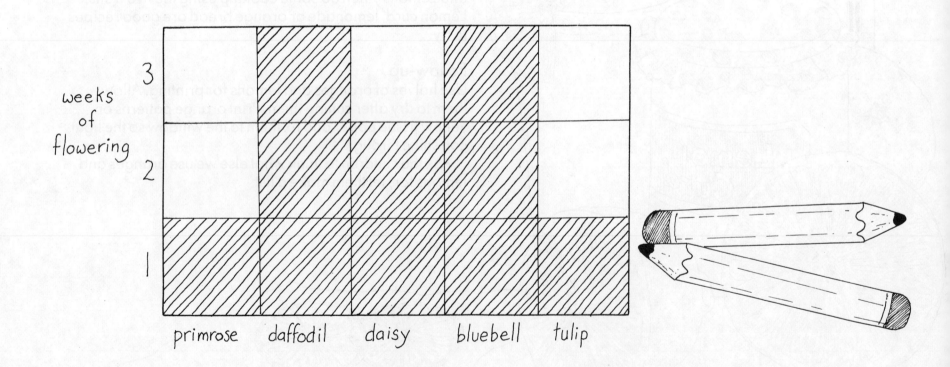

Spring flowers

Age range
Five to seven.

Group size
Whole class, then small groups.

What you need
A collection of pictures of not more than 30 assorted spring flowers, if possible in at least three colours; writing materials.

What to do
Sort the flowers by colour and represent this information pictorially. The children could draw and colour small pictures or cut out and paste ones from magazines. Count the number in each set and discuss and record the numbers obtained, eg three blue flowers, four white flowers, nine yellow flowers, altogether 16 flowers – most yellow ones; fewest blue ones; six more yellow than blue.

Follow-up
Discuss the numbers involved and whether they are odd or even. How do we check whether a number is odd or even? Find the numbers on the number line and give short oral or written tasks, eg 'If we lost our blue flowers how many are left?', 'Has any set an odd number of flowers?', 'How many more flowers would we need to make 20 altogether?'.

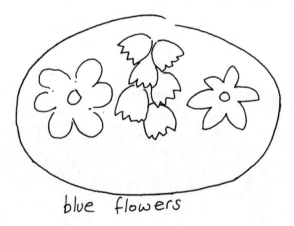

blue flowers

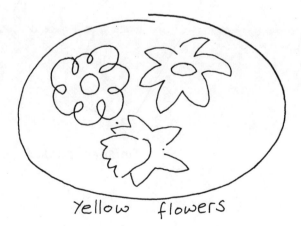

Yellow flowers

white flowers

Spring basket (for infants)

Age range
Five to seven.

Group size
Individuals or small group.

What you need
Coloured paper, a pencil, ruler, scissors, crayons, glue.

What to do
To make each basket, cut a piece of paper as shown and colour a pattern on it. Cut along the solid lines and fold along the dotted lines. Make up the basket as in the diagram, adding a paper handle.

Follow-up
Fill the basket with small sweets for eggs, or make a larger basket and fill it with real or paper flowers.

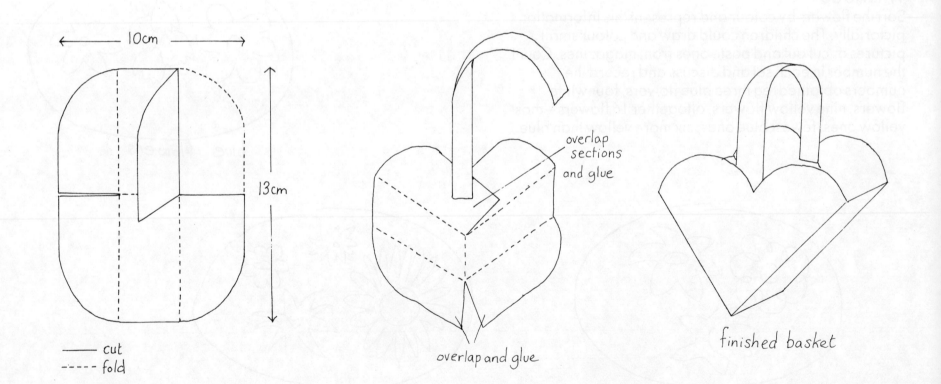

10cm

13cm

——— cut
----- fold

overlap sections and glue

overlap and glue

finished basket

Spring basket (for juniors)

Age range
Seven to nine.

Group size
Individuals.

What you need
Two contrasting colours of paper, a pencil, a ruler, scissors, glue.

What to do
Cut two strips, one from each colour of paper, 7.5×24 cm, and fold them in half. Make two cuts at right angles to the fold, very slightly longer than the width of the strip, and round off the opposite end. Place the two strips at right angles, with the rounded ends facing outwards. Starting with the upper right strip, loop together the three strips, opening out the loops of each half alternately. Cut a handle from another strip of paper and glue it in place.

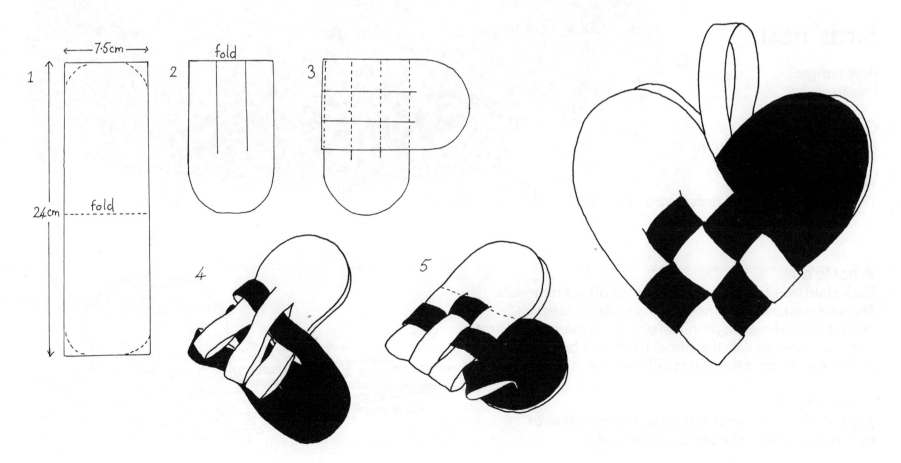

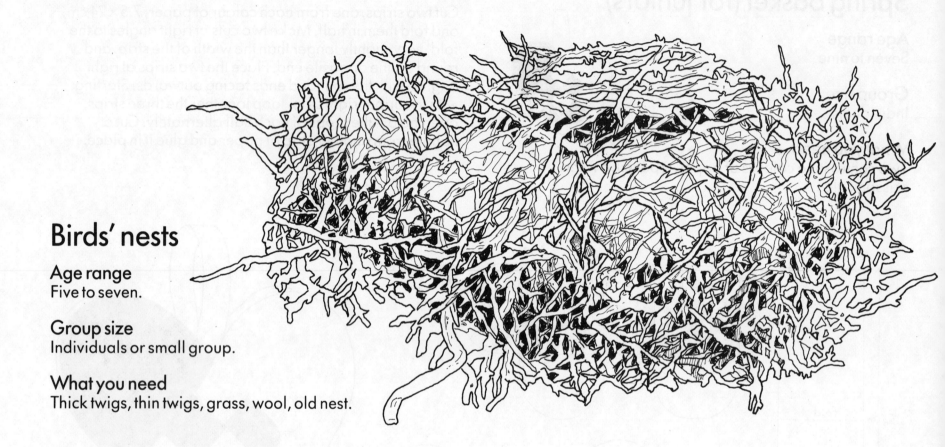

Birds' nests

Age range
Five to seven.

Group size
Individuals or small group.

What you need
Thick twigs, thin twigs, grass, wool, old nest.

What to do
Each child tries to make a nest from the above materials.
The nest must be strong and comfortable. When the
children have finished (or given up!) show them an old nest
and compare this with the models. Which is better?
Remember to bake the nest to kill any insects.

Follow-up
Ask the children to write about their experiences as
nest-builders, then to describe the old nest.

Origami hen

Age range
Nine to eleven.

Group size
Individuals or small group.

What you need
A square of white paper, scissors, glue, paints or crayons.

What to do
Fold the paper as shown in the drawings. Cut out a hen's comb and stick it between the fold on the head. Either colour the hen or splatter paint on it to give a speckled effect.

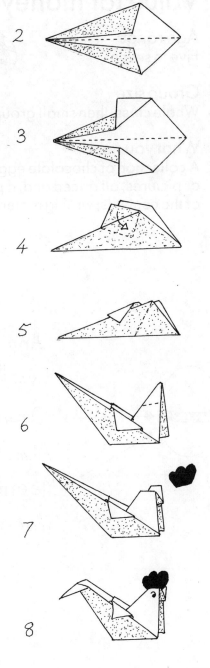

1

2

3

4

5

6

7

8

Value for money

Age range
Five to seven.

Group size
Whole class, then small groups.

What you need
A collection of chocolate eggs, or their empty containers or pictures, all priced and, if possible, showing the weight of the contents; writing materials.

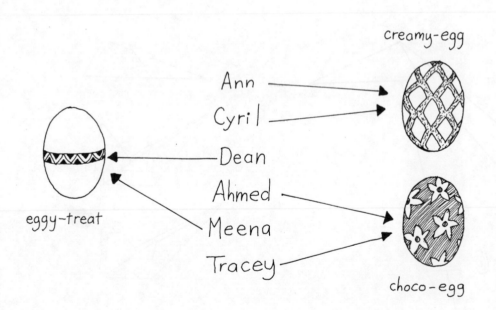

creamy-egg

eggy-treat

choco-egg

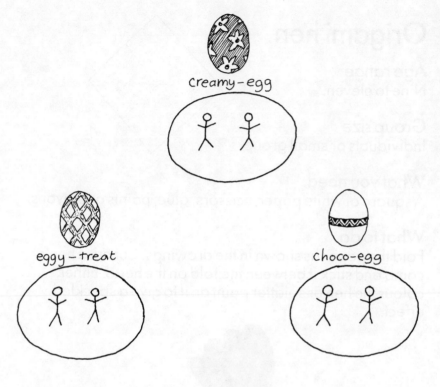

creamy-egg

eggy-treat

choco-egg

What to do
Discuss the collection and chart the answers to the question: 'Which one would you rather have?' This can be a simple mapping or can be done in sets, as shown in the pictures. Then compare the costs and weights and ask children to decide which is the best buy and explain why it is so.

Follow-up
Pose a few problems on chocolate eggs for small groups of two, three or four children, eg 'Mrs Brown has four children and not more than £3 to spend on eggs – how can she spend it fairly?'; 'Could she spend it any other way?' Use the collection for reference for costs, etc.

Three-dimensional egg display

Age range
Seven to eleven.

Group size
Individuals or small group.

plaster filler

What you need
Spoons, cooking oil, plaster of Paris or plaster filler, a knife or ruler, glue, wool, a matchbox, paint, brushes, varnish, scraps of foil, ribbon, paper.

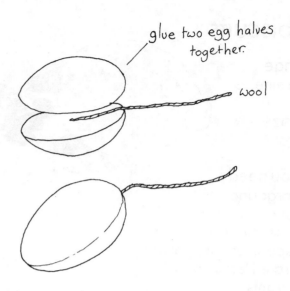

glue two egg halves together.

wool

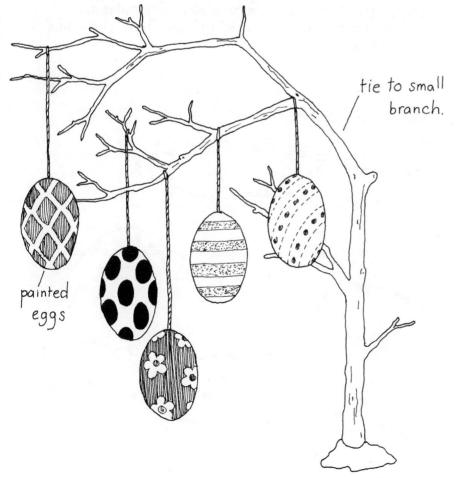

tie to small branch.

painted eggs

What to do
Lightly grease the inside of the spoons. Mix the plaster to a thick, creamy consistency and pour it into the bowl of each spoon. Level the mixture off with the knife or ruler. Leave the plaster-filled spoons overnight, propped in a level position. Next day, invert each spoon and tap it gently on a table until the plaster drops out. Join two egg halves together with strong glue, trapping a piece of wool between them. Fill the seam between the halves with a little wet plaster. Remove any irregularities by rubbing gently with glasspaper or the edge of a matchbox. Paint the eggs with water-colours or powder paint, then varnish and decorate them with scraps of foil, ribbon or sticky paper.

Follow-up
Hang the eggs from a small branch to make a display or decorate half-eggs and glue them to sheets of sugar paper to make a three-dimensional wall display.

  The children could look at birds' eggs or pictures of them, and learn how to identify different eggs. Remember to warn the children not to take eggs from nests.

25

Egg biscuits

Age range
Seven to nine.

Group size
Small group.

What you need
225 g margarine
450 g flour
225 g caster sugar
1 × 5 ml spoon baking powder
a little grated lemon rind
100 g currants
2 eggs
icing

What to do
Rub the margarine into the sifted flour. Add the sugar, baking powder, lemon rind and currants. Mix with the beaten eggs. Roll out to ½ cm thickness and cut into egg-shaped biscuits. Cook for about 20 minutes in a moderate oven, then add an icing bow. These quantities make about 40 biscuits.

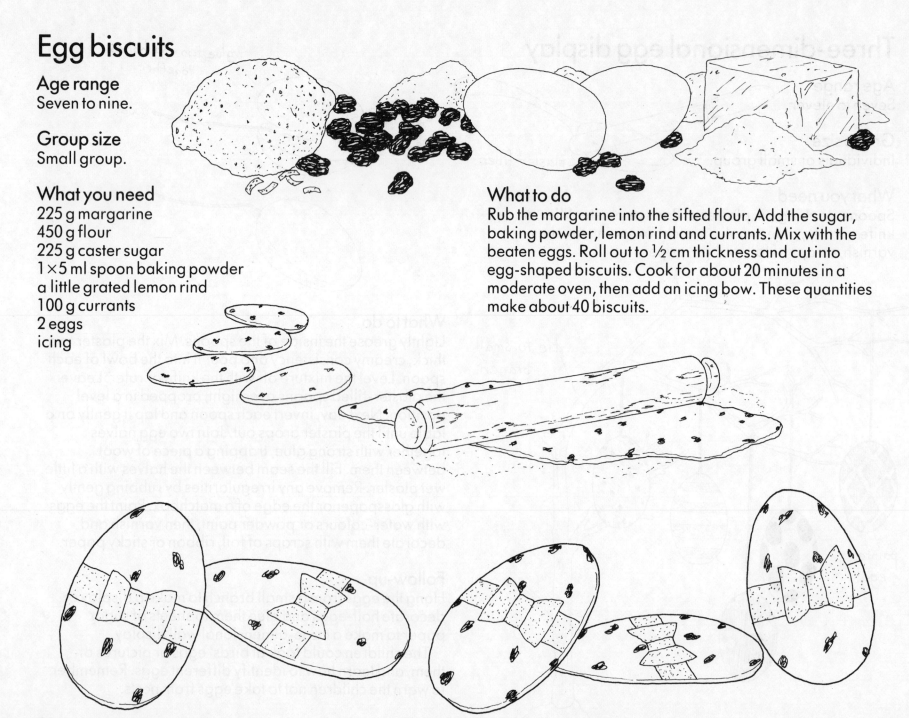

Ordering eggs

Age range
Five to seven.

Group size
Individuals.

What you need
A set of ten cards, each showing a decorated egg of a slightly different size.

What to do
Ask the children to order the eggs. This activity provides a useful check on children's ability to order, especially if the teacher holds back one or two of the cards and asks for them to be inserted in the correct places after the rest have been sorted.

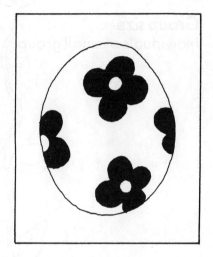

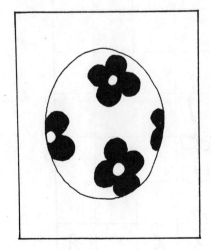

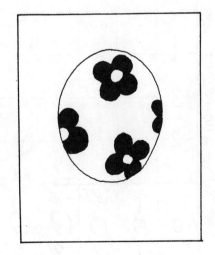

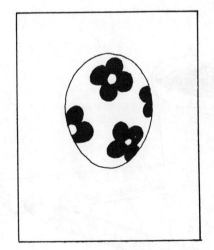

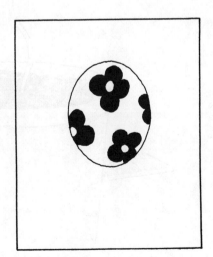

Bean chart

Group size
Individuals or small group.

What you need
Germinating beans, graph paper, writing materials.

What to do
Record each bean's growth by careful observation and measurement. The children can make a graph or block chart showing how their beans grow.

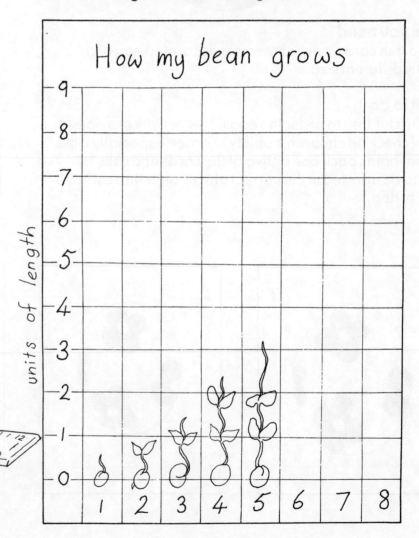

28

Beanometer

Age range
Seven to eleven.

Group size
Small group.

What you need
A bean plant, thin string, drawing pins, an eyelet punch, cardboard, writing materials.

What to do
Make the beanometer as shown. As the bean grows, it allows the string, and therefore the pointer, to move. If the pointer is made to the suggested dimensions, it will magnify the growth ten times.

Follow-up
Plot the position of the pointer at the same time every day and record the results.

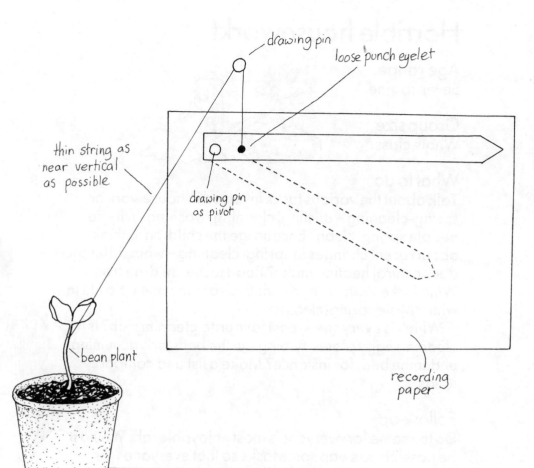

drawing pin

loose punch eyelet

thin string as near vertical as possible

drawing pin as pivot

bean plant

recording paper

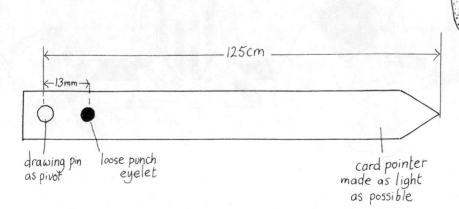

125cm

13mm

drawing pin as pivot

loose punch eyelet

card pointer made as light as possible

Horrible housework!

Age range
Seven to nine.

Group size
Whole class.

What to do
Talk about the various tasks involved in housework or spring-cleaning – dusting, cleaning, washing. Why do people spring-clean? Encourage the children to think about recent changes in spring-cleaning – what difference does central heating make? Read to the children from *Wind in the Willows* by Kenneth Grahame; the episode in which Mole spring-cleans.

Which is everyone's least favourite cleaning job? Is it cleaning eggy plates, wiping out the bath, or vacuuming under the bed, for instance? Make a list and compare ideas.

Follow-up
Do the same for everyone's most enjoyable job. Would it be possible to swap some tasks so that everyone was doing what he/she liked? How could you arrange housework fairly?

Birthdays

Age range
Seven to eleven.

Group size
Whole class, then small groups.

What to do
Refer to Shakespeare's birthday as a starting point and then get all the children to tick the month in which they were born (this could be done under the zodiac signs for a change).

From the numbers obtained, get children to pose questions to each other, eg 'Which month has the most birthdays?', 'How many more in that month than July (or another month)?', 'How many birthdays in spring, summer, autumn, winter?', 'Which season is most popular in our class?', 'Is it the same in other classes?'

Follow-up
In small groups, use information from the main chart and find different ways of displaying the same information, eg block graph, pie chart, sets, mapping, three-dimensionally.

Find the total number of years shown in the class – what is the average age?

Maypoles

Age range
Seven to nine.

Group size
Individuals or small group.

What you need
Twigs or drinking straws, modelling clay, coloured wrapping ribbon, glue.

What to do
To make each maypole, stick the twig or straw into a small piece of modelling clay. Secure strips of coloured wrapping ribbon to the top of the twig or straw. Twist the strips round to form a maypole pattern.

Follow-up
Teach different forms of plaiting. Using different-coloured threads or strips of paper will make it easier for children to see the pattern.

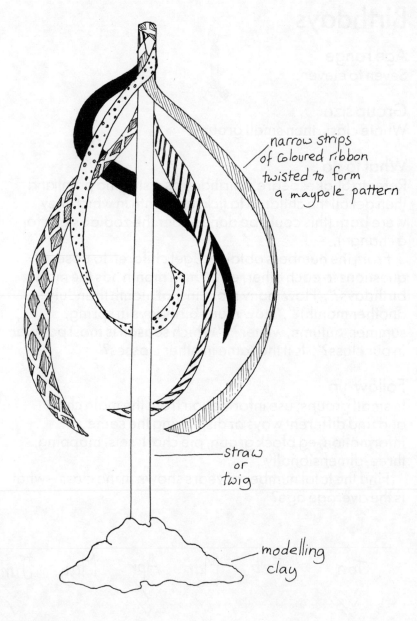

narrow strips of coloured ribbon twisted to form a maypole pattern

straw or twig

modelling clay

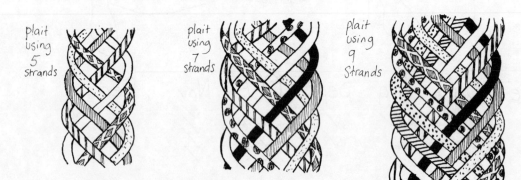

plait using 5 strands

plait using 7 strands

plait using 9 strands

May Day collage

Age range
Seven to nine.

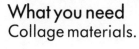

Group size
Small group.

What you need
Collage materials.

What to do
Tell the children about the old May Day custom of young people getting up early and going out into the fields to gather may or hawthorn from trees and hedges. Explain that sometimes the people stayed out overnight, dancing and singing while waiting for the dawn, when they would bring their may boughs home to nail over the doors and windows. This was supposed to bring good luck and ward off witches during the coming year.

The children can then make a large collage showing the custom.

Follow-up
Make a class book of May Day customs. Add any May Day poems or songs you can find.

Discuss the superstition that it is unlucky to bring may blossom indoors. Do the children have any superstitions in their families? Collect these and trace their origins.

Marzipan sweets

Age range
Seven to nine.

Group size
Small group.

What you need
225 g ground almonds
110 g caster sugar
2 drops almond essence
2 egg whites
110 g icing sugar
food dye

What to do
Mix together the almonds, sugar and almond essence. Lightly whisk the egg whites and stir them into the mixture. Turn on to a board dusted with icing sugar and knead until smooth and pliable. Mould into shapes and decorate with food dye.

May lady

Age range
Seven to eleven.

Group size
Whole class.

What you need
Old pairs of tights, sewing materials, newspaper, a coat-hanger, a cane, old clothes or fabric, coloured tissue-paper.

What to do
An old May Day custom was for women and girls to make a figure of a woman and seat it in a chair or under an arch covered with flowers. The figure was dressed prettily and draped with wreaths of flowers. The girls sang special songs as they carried the May lady round, breaking off to say 'Pray remember the poor May lady'. At the end of the procession, the May lady was put at the base of the maypole for the evening's dancing.

   The children can make their own May lady. Make the figure from two pairs of tights, sewing them together across the back of the waistbands. Stuff the legs with newspaper to make the limbs, inserting a coat-hanger across the shoulders. Poke the hook of the hanger through the middle seam. Sew up the waistband. Make the head from the body section of a third pair of tights and sew it to the coat-hanger hook to keep it upright. Dress the figure with cast-off clothes or pieces of material and make a real or tissue-paper flower garland for her head and neck. Construct an arch from a hoop or cane, and cover it with more flowers.

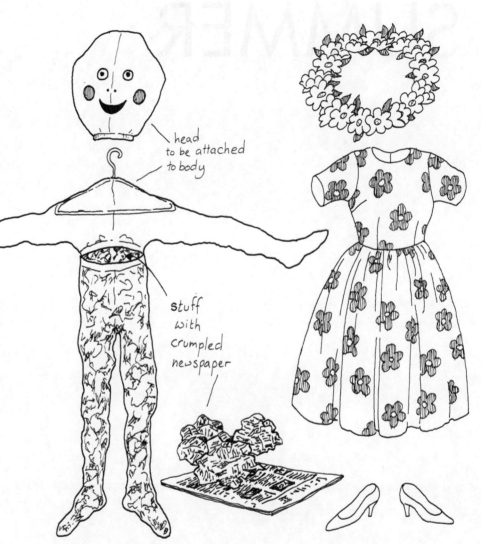

head to be attached to body

stuff with crumpled newspaper

Follow-up
Read the passage from *Lark Rise to Candleford* in which schoolchildren have the day off to take part in a May Day procession.

   Mime a May Day procession, ending with a maypole dance. Make up your own music for the procession.

SUMMER

Displays and collections

Feathers
Shells
Pebbles
Seaweed and sea-shore finds
Things we use to tell the time: clocks, watches,
    egg-timers, sundials, etc
Flowers
Postcards
Stamps
Suitcases and different types of bag
Summer fruits and vegetables
Summer clothing: bathing costumes, sunglasses,
    suntan cream, sandals, sunhats, etc
Summer foods and drinks
Aeroplane, boat or train tickets
Honey
Blue things
Sea-shanties
Summer sports equipment

Topic work

Summer sports
Water sports
The sun
Shadows
Water
Heat
Keeping cool
Travel
Holidays
Aeroplanes and flight
The sea
Fish and fishing
Dairy products
Caravans, boats, tents
Playground and out-of-school games
Picnics
Favourite places
Insects
Imaginary creatures: fairies, gnomes, imps, etc

Summer sports

Age range
Seven to eleven.

Group size
Whole class, then small group.

What you need
Card to make punch cards.

What to do
Having discussed sports generally and homed in on those suited for summer, each child makes a punch card of a favourite sport from the four chosen as favourites.

The child cuts a hole in the top of the card for a favourite sport, then cuts the appropriate boy or girl hole in the top of the card. Remember that the order of the holes must be the same for each individual card.

Follow-up
Make work-cards devised by the children and/or teacher using the punch cards, eg 'How many boys prefer cricket?', 'How many girls prefer tennis?', 'Which sport is top favourite with girls/boys?'

To find how many boys prefer cricket, stick a very fine knitting needle through the cricket hole and another through the boy hole and the cards that fall through will give the required information.

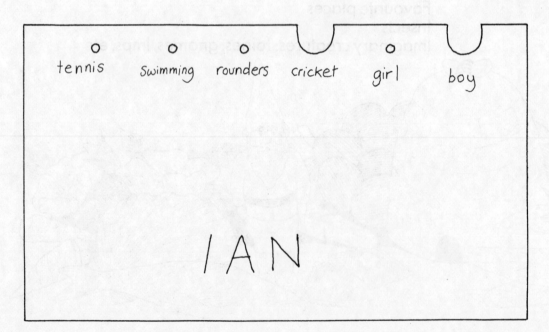

This card shows that the child is a boy and that his favourite sport, from the four given, is cricket.

Tennis-ball pictures

Age range
Five to seven.

Group size
Individuals or small group.

What you need
Old tennis balls, small balls, small bowls, paint, sugar paper, washing-up bowls or round trays, plastic hoops.

What to do
Dampen the balls and roll them round in small bowls of paint until they are thinly coated. Cut the sugar paper into circles to fit the bottom of the washing-up bowls or round trays. Put a ball into each bowl or tray and let the children roll them around to form patterns. Alternatively, place a hoop on a large piece of paper on the floor and let several children sit round it and roll a ball to each other.

Follow-up
Use different colours to produce a pattern. Try bouncing the balls gently to produce splodges rather than lines. Use differently-sized or textured balls to vary the patterns.

round tray lined with paper — tilt the tray to produce a pattern

Grasses

Age range
Seven to eleven.

Group size
Small group.

What to do
Take the children out to see how many different kinds of grass they can find. Take the grasses back to the classroom and measure and compare the lengths of the stems and flower-heads. Look at the arrangement of the flowers. Do they hang down or are they arranged all together to give a single spike-like appearance? Sort the grasses according to different criteria: location, type of flower, stem or head length, etc.

Follow-up
Look in a reference book to find the names of the grasses. Take prints of grasses, mount the prints and label them. Dry some grasses and use them in collages.

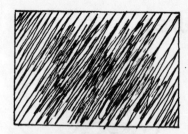

Roll out an area of ink.

Lay grass on ink, cover with newspaper and put a heavy book on top.

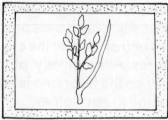

Put a piece of cloth on a table, put printing paper on top and carefully place grass on this.

Cover grass with newspaper and put a heavy book on top.

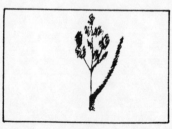

Finished print

Dandelions

Age range
Seven to eleven.

Group size
Small group.

What you need
A trundle wheel, white paper, a hand lens, lint, a transparent plastic box, writing and drawing materials.

What to do
1   Find out how many dandelions are growing on the school field, by measuring the area of the field and counting the plants in a number of sample squares to give an estimate.
2   Observe and draw some of the small animals and insects which visit dandelions, by shaking flowers over white paper and examining them with a lens.
3   Which animals feed on dandelion leaves? Search dandelion plants for evidence.
4   Take about 25 dandelion seeds and put them on damp lint inside a transparent plastic box. Observe them and draw what happens day by day. What percentage of seeds germinate?
5   Count the individual florets on a number of dandelions. Do they all have the same number?
6   Blow dandelion heads as 'clocks'. Talk about seed dispersal and why/how it happens.
7   The dandelion has been called the toughest plant on earth. Test to see if even a very small piece of root left in the ground develops into a new plant.

Follow-up
Collect local names for dandelions: wishes, devil's milk plant, pishmaloog, golden suns, wet weed, etc. Try to explain and find out the origins of these if possible. Taste some dandelion coffee (available from health-food shops) and pick young leaves to make dandelion salad.

Scent panel

Age range
Five to seven.

Group size
Small group.

What you need
Paints, paper, brushes, cotton wool, glue, strong-smelling substances.

What to do
Paint a number of flowers and display them as a frieze. Add centres made from cotton wool soaked in substances with a distinctive smell, such as lemon juice, scent or vinegar. Children can then try to identify the smells with their eyes closed, and draw up a list of preferences/ dislikes. They could make a block graph to show class tastes.

Follow-up
Talk about the importance of a sense of smell. Which animals have a highly-developed sense of smell, and why?

flower shape, painted cut out and mounted on frieze.

come and smell

cotton wool soaked in strong-smelling substances.

Which smell do you like best?
Which smell do you like least?

Well dressing

Age range
Seven to eleven.

Group size
Small group.

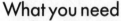

What you need
A collection of cut flowers (including hydrangeas), petals, leaves and grasses, damp clay, a large tray.

What to do
Describe the well dressing which takes place in the villages of the Peak District in Derbyshire – if possible, show children pictures of the decorated wells. Make a collection of small flowers, petals, leaves and grasses. Fill the tray with damp clay and let a small group of children try to make their own decorative flower panel. Stress that they should try to cover all of the clay and that they must work quickly before the clay dries.

A small world

Age range
Seven to eleven.

Group size
Individuals.

What to do
Take children outside to the field. Let them lie down and look through and along the grass, imagining that it is a jungle and that they are very small. Encourage them to imagine that the ants and other insects are ferocious monsters, the flies swooping birds of prey, and the pebbles enormous rocks.

Follow-up
The children can write stories or descriptions of their adventures in the imaginary jungle.

Bees

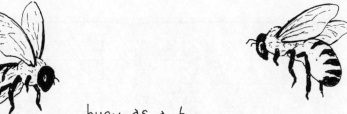

Age range
Nine to eleven.

Group size
Small group.

What you need
Dishes or saucers of different colours, honey or sugar solution.

What to do
Put a dish of honey or sugar solution outside on a table or other observation platform. Once bees have found it, they will return to it regularly. The children can observe the dish to see if the bees have a regular feeding time.

Next, put out the food in containers of different colours. Do the bees have a favourite colour? Make strong and weak solutions of sugar and see if the bees can distinguish between them.

Follow-up
Record the experiments and findings, and display writing around a large bee collage.

Collect sayings about bees and discuss their meanings: 'as busy as a bee', 'make a beeline', 'swarms of people', 'a hive of industry', 'the queen bee'.

Watch bees visiting flowers. With a stop-watch, time how long they stay on each type of flower.

'as busy as a bee'

..... 'make a beeline' .....

'a hive of industry'

'swarms of people'

44

Tomatoes

Age range
Seven to eleven.

Group size
Individuals or small group.

What you need
Seedling tomato plants, grow-bags, writing materials.

What to do
Plant tomato plants in grow-bags and place these against a sunny wall outside school or in a window. Choose plant varieties suitable for growing in these conditions. Give each child or group a tomato plant to look after. Watch these daily and keep diaries of the growth of individual plants, recording the increase in the height of whole shoots, internode growth and leaf length. Keep a few spare seedlings so that you can experiment with keeping a plant in varying amounts of shade or on a restricted amount of water; you can also experiment with different soils and fertilizers. Make observational drawings of the different stages in the seedlings' growth.

Follow-up
Use the tomatoes which the plants produce to make tomato sandwiches.

Midsummer monsters

Age range
Seven to eleven.

Group size
Individuals or small group.

What you need
Old magazines, paper, pencils.

What to do
Discuss how, in the past, it was believed that evil spirits gathered in the darkness. Midsummer's night was chosen as the time to try to get rid of them. Some people thought that the evil spirits took the form of dragons, or fire-drakes, flying about over roof-tops and congregating over rivers, ponds and wells – into which they spat, polluting them, and thus causing the plague and other epidemics rife in medieval times. Discuss what a fire-drake might look like. Children then draw their own fire-drake, and fill the drawings with torn-paper mosaic.

Follow-up
Children do bright paintings of fire-drakes on card, making sure there are no background details. They then cut out the shapes and add texture to them with cotton wool and streamers.

Make a wall poster using frieze paper printed with bright red and orange. Apply the paint with textured rollers bought from an ironmonger. Mount the fire-drake shapes on small boxes, such as matchboxes, and stick them on to the background to give a three-dimensional effect.

Develop some eerie music to accompany a fire-drake's flight.

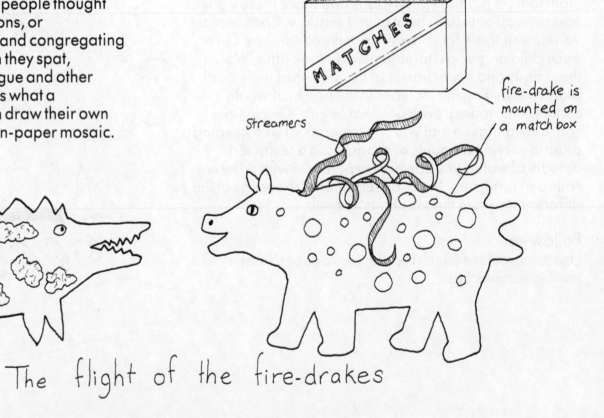

MATCHES

Streamers

fire-drake is mounted on a match box

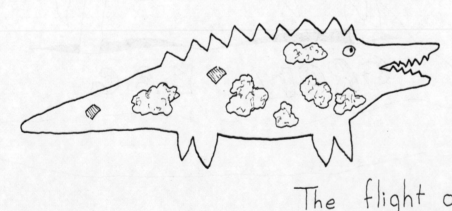

The flight of the fire-drakes

Summer sounds

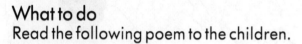

Age range
Seven to nine.

Group size
Small group.

What to do
Read the following poem to the children.

I love the summery
Sounds of June;
A grasshopper chirping
In the drowsy noon;
Fat brown bumble bees
Buzzing by;
A skylark singing,
High up in the sky;
And wood-pigeons cooing
As they go to rest.
These are the sounds
I love the best.

Then discuss the children's favourite summer sounds.

Follow-up
Take the children outside in small groups to close their eyes and listen. What can they hear? They can then make up their own 'summer sounds' poems. This could lead on naturally to considering onomatopoeia and alliteration.

Seaside movement ideas

Age range
Five to seven.

Group size
Large group or whole class.

What you need
A tambourine, suitable music.

What to do

1 The group works as a whole. The children can choose to be anything that lives on the sea-bed: shells, seaweed, sea creatures, etc. All except the sea creatures are rooted to the spot and must use hands, arms and legs to suggest movement: the seaweed waves gently, the shells open and catch small fish before closing, the rocks make tall spiky shapes. The sea creatures move slowly and carefully around the other children.

2 The children work individually. They mime walking on hard sand and on soft sand, then on a pebbly beach. Use a tambourine to indicate light movements over hard sand and heavy movements over soft sand.

3 The children work in two groups: shells or pebbles, and sea. The pebbles take up their position on the beach, then the sea rushes up and moves them along the sand. The pebbles roll back a little with the back-wash.

4 Divide the class into two groups: one is a family and the other the sea. The family falls asleep and the sea gradually encircles them and cuts them off. The children work out a sequence to show what the family do and how they are rescued.

5 The children work individually miming the following: digging in the sand, making sand-castles, brushing sand off their hands and feet, letting sand trickle through their fingers.

Sea-shore treasures

Age range
Seven to nine.

Group size
Whole class.

What you need
A cardboard or wooden box (or, if you have one, an old, interesting chest), sea-shore items, card, writing materials.

What to do
Decorate the box to make a treasure chest. Place interesting seaside treasures – pebbles, starfish, shells, etc – inside. The children dip into the box without looking, take an item, then write a story, description or poem about it. Attach a small card to each item, giving relevant words to stimulate the children's ideas.

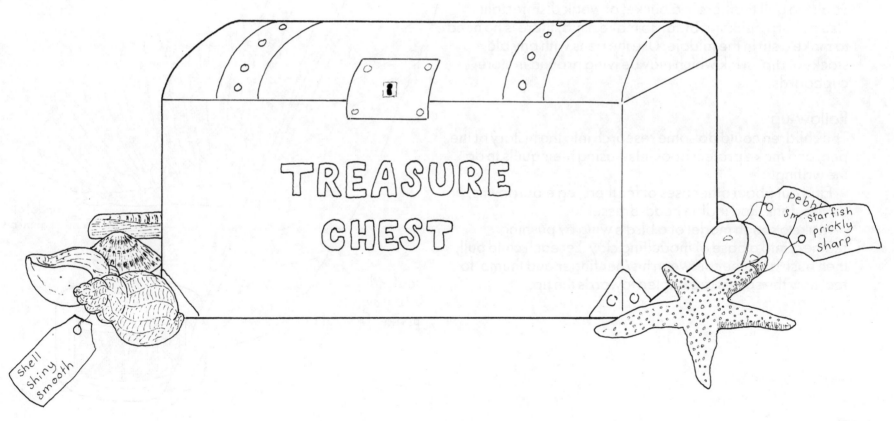

TREASURE CHEST

Shell Shiny Smooth

Pebbl Sm starfish prickly sharp

Gull feathers

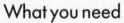

Age range
Seven to eleven.

Group size
Individuals or small group.

What you need
Gull feathers, a bucket, disinfectant, a penknife, ink.

What to do
Soak the gull feathers in a bucket of weak disinfectant.
Use a sharp penknife blade to make a nib; there is no need
to make a slit in the middle. Use the pens with any old
stocks of dip-in ink which may be lying around in store
cupboards.

Follow-up
The children could do some research into the history of the
pen, and make project booklets – using their quills to do
the writing!

Find out about other uses of feathers, eg eiderdowns,
duvets, fans, Red Indian head-dresses.

Make a rough model of a bird's wing by pushing
feathers into a base of modelling clay. Let each child pull,
then push a feather between his/her finger and thumb, to
feel how the spines are angled towards the tip.

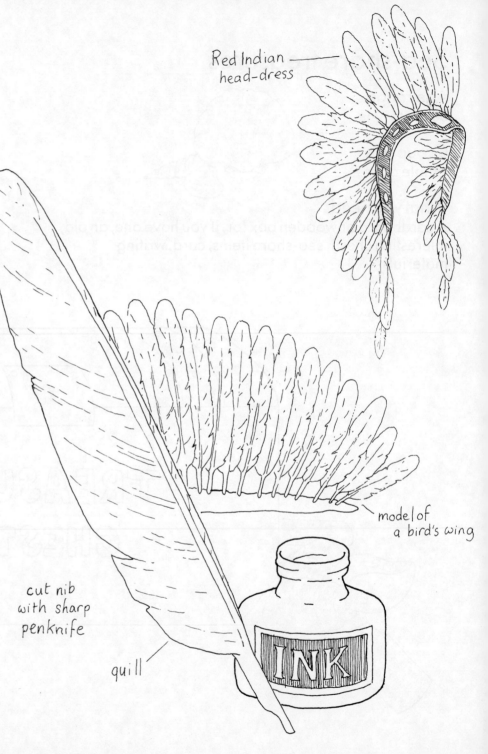

Red Indian head-dress

model of a bird's wing

cut nib with sharp penknife

quill

INK

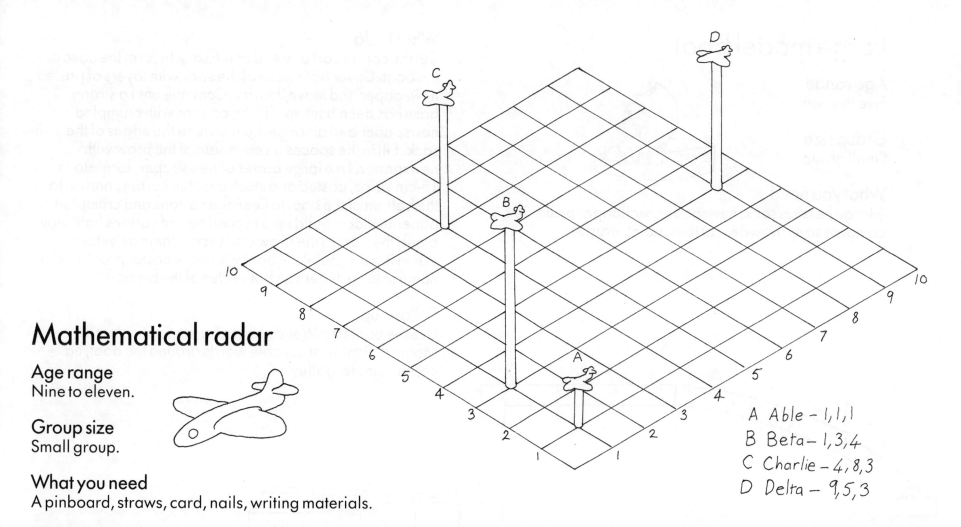

A Able – 1, 1, 1
B Beta – 1, 3, 4
C Charlie – 4, 8, 3
D Delta – 9, 5, 3

Mathematical radar

Age range
Nine to eleven.

Group size
Small group.

What you need
A pinboard, straws, card, nails, writing materials.

What to do
The pinboard represents an area of ground on the approach to an airport. Draw a grid on the pinboard, and mark on co-ordinates as shown, having first discussed a realistic scale. Cut the straws to different lengths to represent different heights above ground. Cut scraps of card into small aeroplane shapes and stick them to one end of the straws. The other end of each straw can then be slotted over a nail or pin on the board.

Follow-up
Find the position of the aircraft in the air, using three co-ordinates – north, west and height. Plot courses from different parts of the board in order to land at the edge of the board. Practise talking down an aeroplane to avoid a collision, and talk about the practice of 'stacking' aircraft which are awaiting landing permission.

Large model boat

Age range
Five to seven.

Group size
Small group.

What you need
A large hessian sack, newspaper, wallpaper paste, 30 cereal or soap-powder cartons, paint, brushes.

What to do
Cut the corners off one end of the sack to form the base of the boat. Cover both sides of the sack with layers of pasted newspaper and leave it to dry. Continue until a strong base has been built up. Fill the cartons with crumpled newspaper and arrange them around the edges of the sack. Fill in the spaces on each side of the prow with newspaper. Use large pages of newspaper, torn into 15-cm strips, pasted and stuck over the cartons and on to the bottom of the boat to keep the cartons and crumpled paper in place. Build up a second row of cartons half-way along the boat to the prow and secure them as before. When it is dry, paint the boat with thick poster paint. Add a name in large letters on both sides of the prow.

Follow-up
Use the boat as a Wendy house for summer role-play. Mount a display of suitable words around the boat, eg captain, mate, galley.

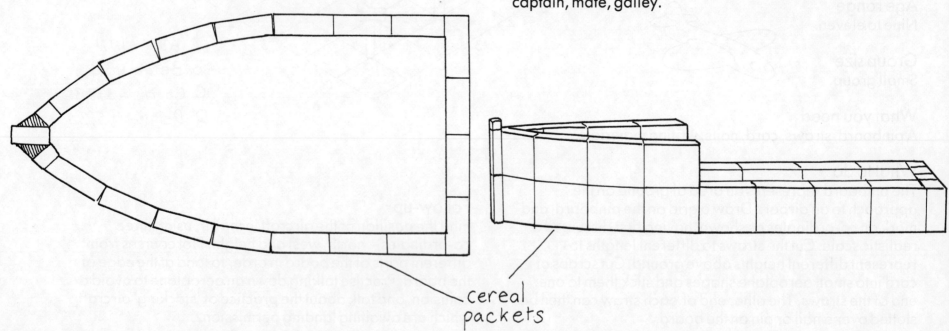

cereal packets

Investigating boats

Age range
Five to seven.

Group size
Whole class, then small group.

What you need
A large model boat, as described on page 52 (or one made from bricks, chairs, tables), some non-standard units of measure, metre sticks, writing materials, painting materials.

What to do
Find out how many children can stand, sit, lie down in the boat. Discuss various non-standard measures that could be used to find out the length and width of the boat, eg hand spans, foot lengths, children lying prone, Unifix cubes. Record some of the findings pictorially.

Follow-up
Discuss which unit was easiest to use and which the most difficult. Lead on to the idea of a standard unit; use a metre stick and record: 'Our boat is more than four sticks long but less than five', 'Our boat is more than two sticks and less than three sticks wide'. Discuss half metres and the concept of 'about'.

A hard sell

Age range
Seven to eleven.

Group size
Individuals.

What you need
Travel agents' brochures, card or thick paper, writing and colouring materials.

What to do
Look through the brochures to see how the companies try to sell holiday locations. Children then make their own brochures, of a familiar place such as the recreation ground, local park, swimming pool, market or museum. Make the brochures in concertina form, with six pages.

1 Picture and title page.
2 How to get there: a simple map and a description of the route.
3 Things to see and do: drawings and descriptions.
4 A story connected with the location, or an account of a day spent there.
5 Fares or admission charges, the time of the journey and things to look out for on the way.
6 Descriptive writing to sell the idea that this is a good place to visit.

Follow-up
Display and read each others' brochures. The children decide which place they would most like to visit on the basis of its brochure.

Make a cardboard TV, as shown in the diagram, and design advertisements to feed through the screen to sell the idea further.

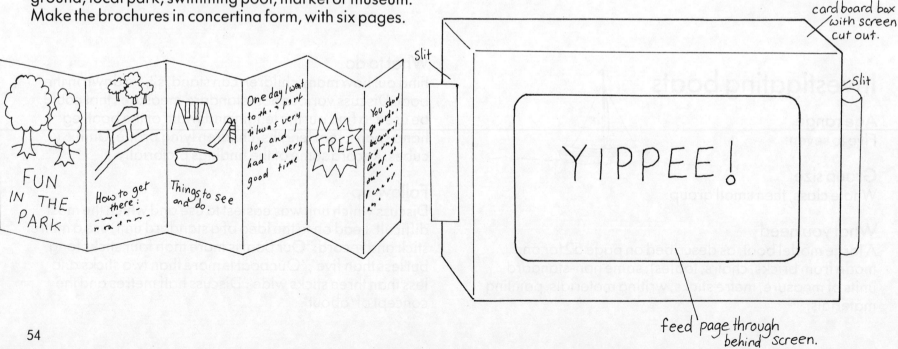

Choosing a holiday

Age range
Seven to eleven.

Group size
Individuals.

What you need
Travel agents' brochures (ask travel agents whether they have any old ones).

What to do
The children pretend they have won £350 in a holiday competition. They look through the brochures and decide which holiday they would choose, then give their reasons for choosing that holiday.

Follow-up
What will the children need extra money for? How much more money will they need? Will £350 be enough? Again using the brochures, work out the cost of holidays for families of three, four and five people in different countries and hotels.

Caravans

Age range
Five to nine.

Group size
Whole class.

What you need
Sleeping-bags, assorted cartons, boxes, tins.

What to do
Turn your home corner into a caravan – bring in some old sleeping-bags for children to act out unrolling them at night time and rolling them up again during the day. Set up a caravan-site shop and discuss what will need to be sold – newspapers, tea, milk, coffee, sugar, cornflakes, meat, vegetables, fruit, comics, books, sweets, etc. Use old cartons, tins and boxes to stock the shop – cylindrical tins painted blue make good Calor-gas refills!

Follow-up
Plan a caravan site and discuss the best place for a shop. Work out how to position it so that it is equidistant from all parts of the site.

Talk about and collect pictures of different types of caravans – gypsy caravans, circus caravans, mobile homes, etc.

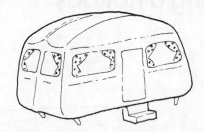

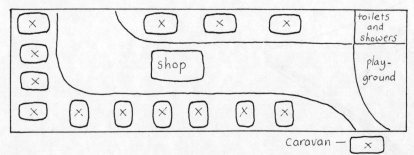

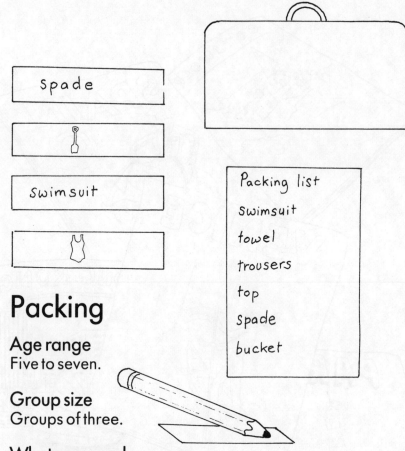

Packing

Age range
Five to seven.

Group size
Groups of three.

What you need
Small boxes or tins, card, writing materials.

What to do
Use the tins or boxes, suitably covered, to represent suitcases or cut suitcase shapes from card. Make a list of items to be packed in each suitcase. Make a small card for each item, with a picture on one side and the word on the other.

The children have suitcases and lists. They collect cards to go with the items on their lists, and 'pack' them in their suitcases.

Postcards

Age range
Five to nine.

Group size
Individuals.

What you need
Rulers, thin card, old magazines or travel brochures, paste, scissors, pencils, sticky paper, a pin.

What to do
Cut out pieces of cardboard 13×8 cm. Children look through the magazines or brochures for pictures that will fit the cards and paste them on to the cards. Then they turn the cards over, draw a line down the centre and print the word 'postcard' at the top. They write their friend's name and address on the right-hand side and a message on the left-hand side.

To make stamps, fold a piece of sticky paper, 12×9 cm, in half twice each way to make 16 small rectangles. Open out the paper and prick holes through the creases with a pin, so that individual stamps can be torn off when required. Alternatively, use an unthreaded sewing machine to make the perforations.

Follow-up
The stamps can be sold in the class shop. Post the cards in a class post-box and appoint a member of class to be the postman or postwoman.

POSTCARD

Dear John,
It is lovely here. The sun is hot and I have been swimming.
with love
from Mina

John Smith
Class 2
All Saints' School

pin or needle holes

Sticky paper

Sky picture

Age range
Seven to nine.

Group size
Small group.

What to do
After reading this poem to the children, take them outside
to look at the clouds and make up their own sky pictures.
Repeat this on different days to get contrasting views of
the clouds.

I looked up one day at the bright summer sky,
And watched the great clouds floating lazily by,
And suddenly there was no sky any more,
But a calm, turquoise sea and a magical shore!

There were islands all silver, mysterious caves,
And a beach of pure gold stretching down to the waves.
Through pale shreds of mist stealing over the scene,
Great mountains were rising, snow-capped and serene.

White seagulls swooped down, and would silently rest
And rock themselves gently upon the sea's breast.
A ship rode at anchor, sails billowing wide,
As she waited offshore for the turn of the tide.

As I gazed on the scene, how I wished I could be
On that long, sandy beach by the glittering sea!
But a dark cloud passed over the face of the sun,
And my lovely sky picture was faded and done!

All sorts of weather

Age range
Five to seven.

Group size
Large group or whole class.

What to do
The words should be spoken in strict rhythm while the children mime the action.

Teacher: How do little showers come?
Children: Patter, patter, patter, patter.
Teacher: How does heavy rain fall?
Children: Flop, flop, flop, flop.
Teacher: What d'you think the thunder says?
Children: Bang! bang! bang! bang!
Teacher: How d'you think the lightning goes?
Children: Flash! flash! flash! flash!
All: And then a big *crash*!

59

Paper sun

Age range
Seven to nine.

Group size
Individuals or small group.

What you need
Yellow or orange paper, a lampshade ring or small hoop, pencils, glue, cotton.

What to do
To make each sun, cut a circle of paper, place the ring or hoop in the centre and draw round its inner edge. Cut into the paper circle as far as the inner circle to make a number of even sections. Tie a cotton thread to the ring or hoop, then slip it between alternate sections of the circle and glue it in place.

Follow-up
Make a number of suns, then suspend them to form a mobile.

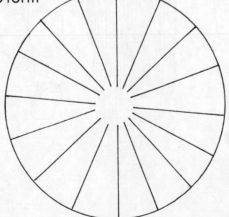

What does the sun do?

Age range
Five to seven.

Group size
Small group or whole class.

What you need
Dolls' clothes, tea-towels or scraps of fabric, washing powder, bowls or sinks, a washing line, watches or clocks, writing materials.

What to do
Help the children to wash and rinse the dolls' clothes, tea-towels or fabric. Hang one item to dry in the sun and another in the shade; leave another on the ground, and another screwed up in the sun. Then time them to see how quickly each item dries. Compare the results. Which dries most quickly/slowly? Would the items dry if they were hung up indoors?

Follow-up
Record the experiment and the children's findings with captioned pictures.

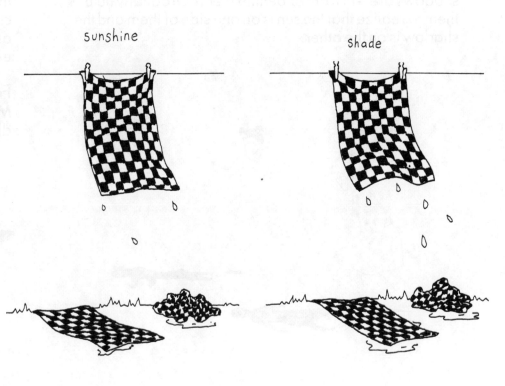

sunshine

shade

Which tea-towel dried most quickly?
Which tea-towel dried most slowly?

Shadows

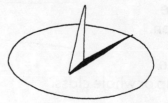

Age range
Five to nine.

Group size
Large group or whole class.

What to do
Take the children outside on a sunny day. Tell them to try to run away from their shadows.

Follow-up
Ask the children to look and see where each others' shadows are – in front or behind them? Gradually help them to realize that the sun is on one side of them and the shadow is on the other.

Comparing shadows

Age range
Five to nine.

Group size
Small group.

What you need
A large sheet of paper, a pen, a tape-measure.

What to do
Take a large sheet of paper outside in the morning, and 'catch' a child's shadow on it. Draw round the shadow, measure its height and compare this with the height of the child. Do the same in the afternoon. Cut out both shadows and compare them. Why aren't they the same size? Is either the same height as the child?

Follow-up
Mount the shadows and the children's findings as a wall display.

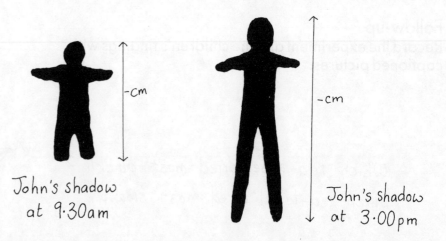

John's shadow at 9.30am

John's shadow at 3.00pm

Summer food

Age range
Five to nine.

Group size
Whole class, then small group.

What you need
A collection of pictures of summer food and drink, writing materials.

What to do
Discuss and compare the foods we enjoy in summer and winter. Talk about drinks; get the children to choose their favourite summer drink and their favourite dessert. Let the children work in two groups, one to make a block graph of favourite drinks, the other of favourite desserts.

Use the numbers involved for comparisons, addition, finding on the number line, etc.

Follow-up
Make jellies in three or four different-sized containers. Discuss conservation of liquid and follow this up during water play. Divide the jellies equally between the class, using dessertspoonfuls as the measure. How many spoonfuls each? How many altogether?

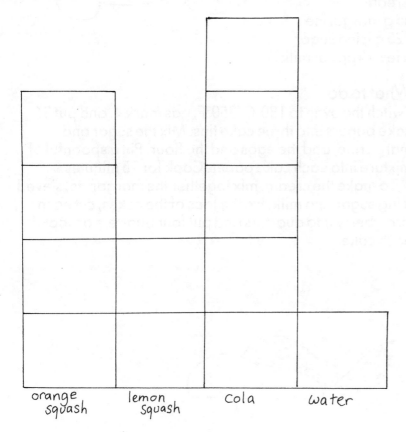

favourite drinks

favourite desserts

63

Summer fruit cooking

Age range
Five to eleven.

Group size
Small group.

Strawberry creams

What you need
36 strawberries
180 g margarine
180 g sugar
3 big eggs
225 g flour
a few drops of milk
36 cake papers

Cream :
55 g margarine
225 g icing sugar
a few drops of milk

What to do
Switch the oven to 180°C/350°F, gas mark 4, and put 36 cake papers into three cake tins. Mix the sugar and margarine, add the eggs and the flour. Put a spoonful of mixture into each cake paper. Cook for 15 minutes.

To make the cream, mix together the margarine, sieved icing sugar and milk. Ice the tops of the cakes, cut each strawberry into quarters and put four quarters on top of each cake.

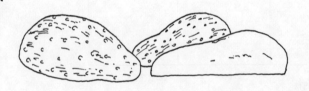

Cherry trifles

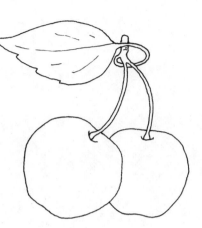

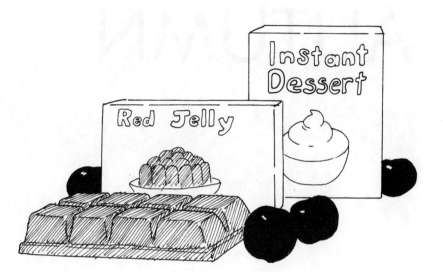

What you need
1 large, jam Swiss roll (bought)
3 packets red jelly
1 kg cooked and stoned cherries
2 packets of
Instant Whip
2 pints milk
36 paper jelly-dishes

What to do
Dissolve the jelly in a little boiling water and add cold water to make it up to the amount specified on the packet. Leave the jellies to set – perhaps you could make them the day before – and then cut the Swiss roll into 18 slices. Put half a slice into each dish, share out the cherries, the Instant Whip and the jelly between each dish, and put the dishes in a cold place to set.

Follow-up
The children can write about what they did.

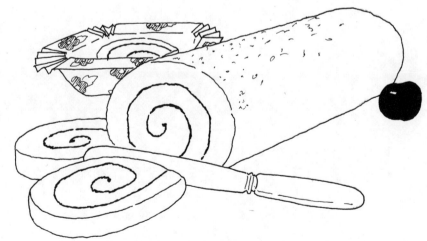

AUTUMN

Displays and collections

Fruits and vegetables
Food labels and packets with country of origin
Seeds
Leaves
Bark
Bread
Types of corn and corn products
Apples
Bulbs
Nuts
Corn dollies
Lamps, candles, matches
Brown, red and orange things
Brushes
Baskets

Topic work

Farming
Harvest
Food – from planting to eating
Deciduous and evergreen trees
Hibernation
Witches and wizards
Superstitions
Guy Fawkes
Fire
Night
Bird migration
Cats
Spiders and creepy-crawlies
Scotland
Poppies
Our school
Food

Harvest festival

Age range
Seven to eleven.

Group size
Whole class.

What to do
Discuss the autumn fairs held in rural England in the past, when servants would hire themselves to new masters. Each servant carried a symbol indicating the type of work he/she did: a mop for a maidservant, a wisp of wool for a shepherd, etc.

Ask the children to think up symbols that people might carry today. How would a computer programmer indicate his or her job? Or an airline pilot? Or a schoolteacher?

Follow-up
Make a large frieze of an autumn fair, showing the servants and their symbols.

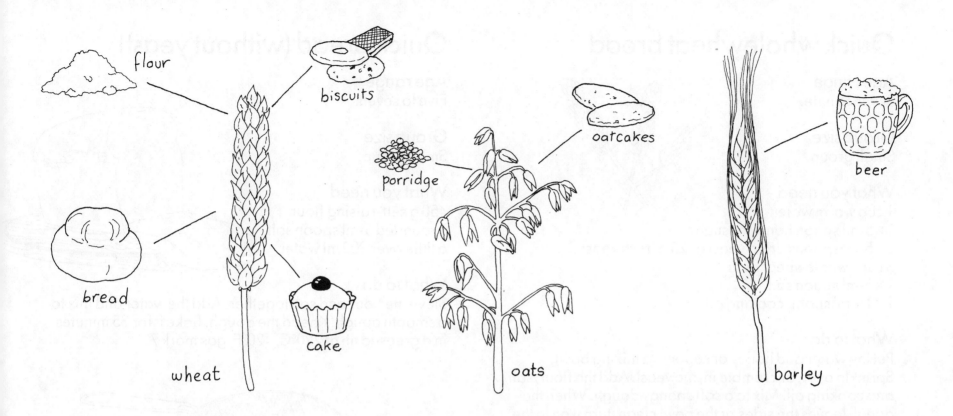

flour

biscuits

oatcakes

porridge

beer

bread

cake

wheat

oats

barley

Corn

Age range
Seven to nine.

Group size
Individuals or whole class.

What you need
Fresh grains or ears of wheat, oats and barley (try a farmer, corn merchant or pet-food shop), pieces of flannel.

What to do
Discuss the different foods which are made from the grains.

Lay the grains on pieces of wet flannel and leave them at normal room temperature. Keep the flannel wet and the seeds should sprout in a day or two. By the end of the week, each grain should also have three roots and a stalk shoot. Plant them in small pots.

Follow-up
Display grains of corn in small plastic bags, surrounded by pictures or labels of foods made from them.

Keep a diary of the growth patterns of the various grains of corn, with regular observational drawings.

Quick wholewheat bread

Age range
Seven to nine.

Group size
Small group.

What you need
1 cup warm water
1×5-ml spoon honey or sugar
3×5-ml spoons dried yeast or 25 g fresh yeast
3 cups wholewheat flour
1×5-ml spoon salt
1×15-ml spoon cooking oil

What to do
Put the water and honey or sugar in a mixing bowl.
Sprinkle over, or crumble in, the yeast. Add the flour, salt
and cooking oil. Mix to a soft spongy dough. When the
dough leaves the sides of the bowl clean, turn it on to the
table. Knead it for two or three minutes, then shape it to fit
and put it in the loaf tin. Brush the top with salty water. Put
the tin in a polythene bag and leave the dough to prove in
a warm place until it has doubled in size. Bake at 230°C,
450°F or gas mark 8 for about 30 minutes.

Follow-up
Explain how yeast works.

Quick bread (without yeast)

Age range
Five to seven.

Group size
Small group.

What you need
450 g self-raising flour
1 rounded 5-ml spoon salt
a little over 300 ml water

What to do
Sieve the flour and salt together. Add the water and mix to
a smooth dough. Knead the dough. Bake it for 35 minutes
in a greased tin at 220°C, 420°F, gas mark 7.

Harvest wheatsheaf

Age range
Seven to eleven.

Group size
Small group.

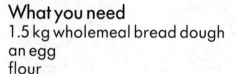

What you need
1.5 kg wholemeal bread dough
an egg
flour

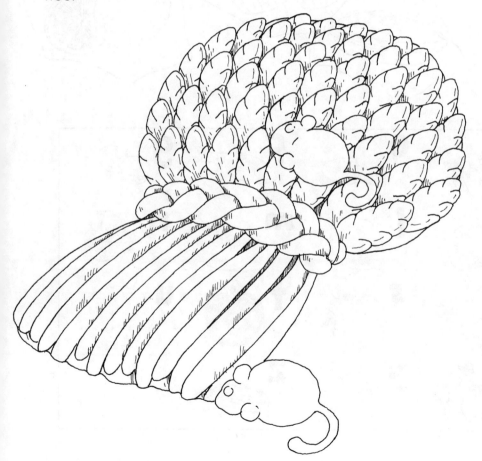

What to do
A harvest wheatsheaf can be made and modelled in
school, then cooked at home. It would make a lovely
addition to a Harvest Festival.

Knead the dough until smooth, then cut off
approximately one third. Roll out the third to fit the baking
tray; cut and push it into a wheatsheaf shape. Make sure
the baking tray is well greased. Give each child a piece of
the remaining dough about the size of a walnut. Some can
make ears, others can make stalks. To make an ear,
knead the piece until it is smooth and roll it with the palm of
the hand on the table, pressing a little more at one end
than the other to make a bullet shape. Press it gently and,
with scissors, snip diagonally towards the centre. For
stalks, roll the dough between the palm of the hand and
the table to form long worm shapes. Brush the shape on
the tray with beaten egg and lay the ears and stalks on it so
that they appear natural. Some children will enjoy making
little harvest mice to lie on the base of the sheaf. The sheaf
is finished off with a plait which encircles the waist. Make
three worms of about the same length and thickness and
plait them. Brush the whole shape with egg and put it into a
hot oven. Reduce the heat after the first five minutes and
cook slowly until golden brown and firm. Cool on a rack.

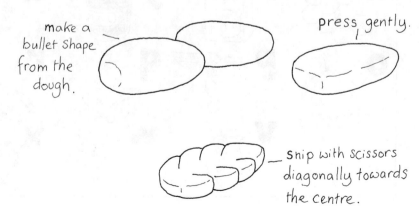

make a bullet shape from the dough.

press gently.

snip with scissors diagonally towards the centre.

Food alphabet

Age range
Five to seven.

Group size
Whole class.

What to do
Make up a food alphabet: a for apple, b for banana, c for custard, etc. Find a picture for each item and mount them as a frieze.

Follow-up
Read to the children from *Rebecca's World* by Terry Nation.

Make up a word bank on food and use it as the basis for writing work.

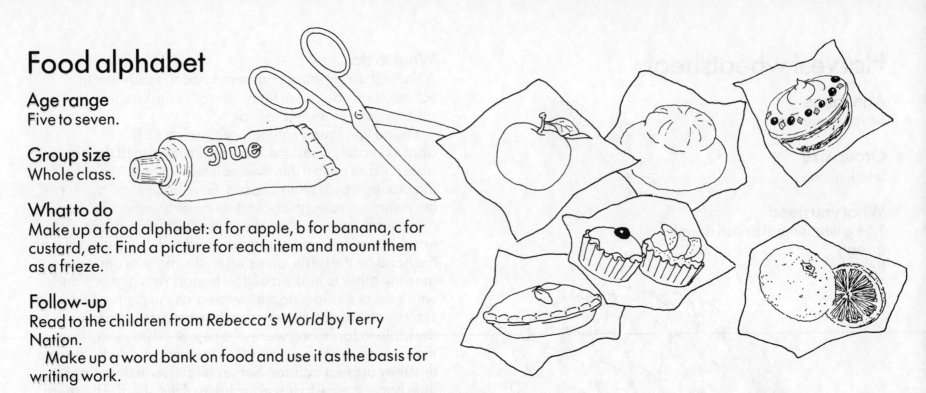

What is behind the door?

Age range
Five to seven.

Group size
Whole class, then individuals.

What you need
A food alphabet frieze (as on page 72), pastel - coloured paper, pens.

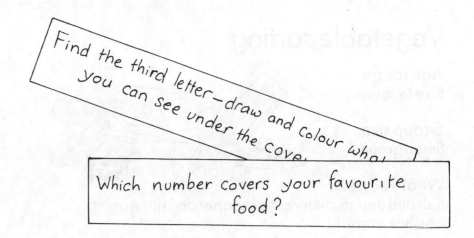

Find the third letter—draw and colour what you can see under the cover.

Which number covers your favourite food?

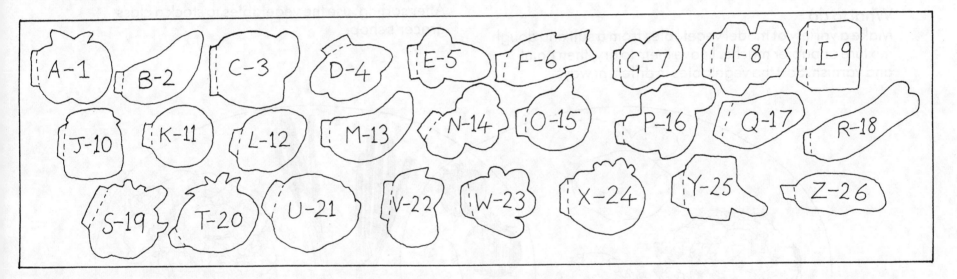

A-1 B-2 C-3 D-4 E-5 F-6 G-7 H-8 I-9

J-10 K-11 L-12 M-13 N-14 O-15 P-16 Q-17 R-18

S-19 T-20 U-21 V-22 W-23 X-24 Y-25 Z-26

What to do
Discuss the alphabet frieze. Suggest that each letter needs a door or cover to hide it. Involve as many children as practicable in cutting out and colouring 26 covers, one to fit over each picture. These are then labelled A to Z and also numbered 1 to 26. Discuss the shape of the cover, and also how to cut the size required economically from a larger sheet.

Follow-up
Oral instructions or work-cards give the following tasks: Find the third letter – draw and colour what you can see under the cover. What can you find under the ninth cover? Which number covers your favourite food? Draw the food next to the last number, etc.

Vegetable sorting

Age range
Five to seven.

Group size
Small group.

What you need
Salt and dough mixture, newspaper and glue, paint, brushes, varnish.

What to do
Make a variety of model vegetables from a salt and dough mixture or papier mâché. Leave them to dry, then paint and varnish. Sort the vegetables in different ways.

1   Those which grow under/above the earth.
2   Those the children like/don't like.
3   Those which are eaten raw/cooked – discuss which set the vegetables belong to if they can be eaten either raw or cooked, and introduce the intersection of sets.
4   According to the part of the plant we eat (stems – celery; leaves – spinach, lettuce, cabbage, kale, cress; roots, tubers, bulbs – carrots, potatoes, turnips, onions, parsnips; seeds – broad beans, peas).
5   Those we peel/don't peel.

Follow-up
After sorting, use the vegetables to stock a class grocer's shop.

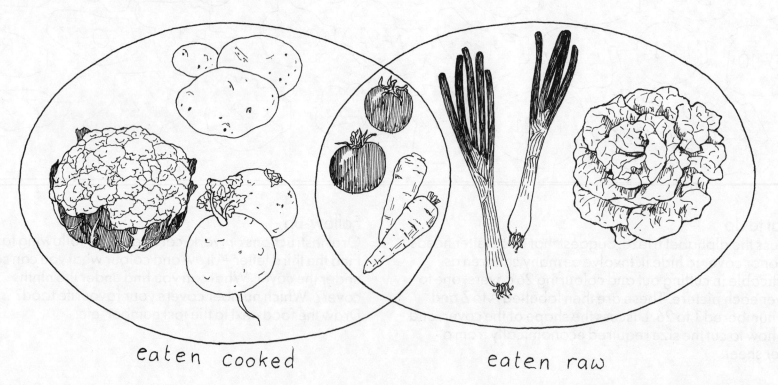

eaten cooked   eaten raw

apples
melon
new potatoes
cauliflowers
grapes

Best buy

Age range
Seven to nine.

Group size
Small group.

What to do
The children find out which fruits and vegetables are in season by looking in local shops. Are the fruits and vegetables grown in Britain or imported?

Price the fruits and vegetables from several shops and prepare a best-buy chart.

Discuss and make lists describing good-quality fruit and vegetables, eg apples – unblemished, crisp, firm.

Follow-up
Plot the price variations of foods over several weeks.

Bloodhounds

Age range
Five to seven.

Group size
Small group.

What you need
Jars, seasonal fruits and vegetables, a blindfold.

What to do
Put small portions of the fruits and vegetables in jars. The children are blindfolded in turn, and try to identify each food by its smell. Who is the best bloodhound?

Follow-up
Develop a word bank to describe the different smells.

Apple action rhymes

Age range
Five to seven.

Group size
Small group or whole class.

Apples, apples, one, two, three,
Apples for you,
Apples for me.
Apples big,
Apples small,
Apple trees tiny,
Apple trees tall.
Apples sour,
Apples sweet,
Apples, apples, are nice to eat.

Five rosy apples by the cottage door,
One tumbled off the twig, then there were four.

Four rosy apples hanging on the tree,
The farmer's wife took one and then there were three.

Three rosy apples; what shall I do?
I think I'll have one, then there'll be two.

Two rosy apples hanging in the sun;
You have the big one; that will leave one.

One rosy apple, soon it is gone;
The wind blew it off the branch; now there is none!

Apple-tree frieze

Age range
Five to seven.

Group size
Small group.

What you need
A few apples, a large sheet of paper for background, paint, brushes, collage materials, red and green foil, fabric, crayons, scissors, glue.

What to do
Let the children look carefully at the apples and help them to observe the apples' shape and colour. Draw several large skeleton tree shapes on a background. Fill these in with paint or prints. Each child then draws and cuts out an apple and leaf shape and decorates it with the materials of his or her choice (foil, fabric, crayon, paint, etc). The finished apples are stuck on the trees.

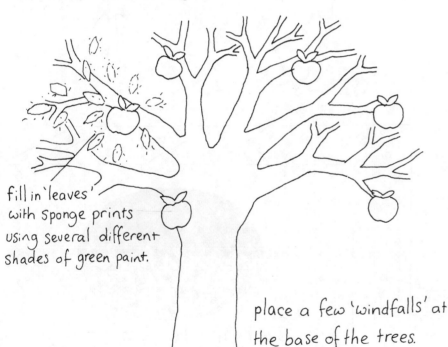

fill in 'leaves' with sponge prints using several different shades of green paint.

place a few 'windfalls' at the base of the trees.

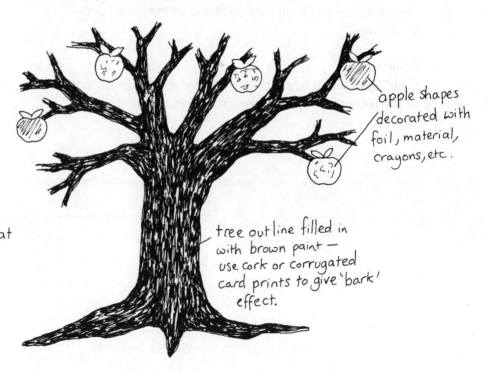

apple shapes decorated with foil, material, crayons, etc.

tree outline filled in with brown paint — use cork or corrugated card prints to give 'bark' effect.

Scrunch box

Age range
Five to nine.

Group size
Whole class.

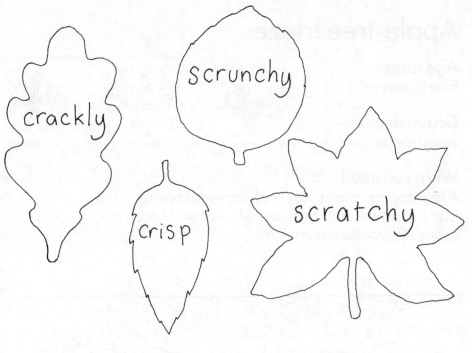

What you need
A strong cardboard box, dry autumn leaves.

What to do
Cut a hole in the side of the box. Cover the box with wallpaper, leaving the hole free. Fill the box with leaves. The children put their hands through the hole to feel the leaves.

Follow-up
Build up a word bank of tactile words, describing the feel of the leaves. Display them above the scrunch box.

Leaf sandwiches

Age range
Five to nine.

Group size
Individuals or small group.

What you need
Colourful autumn leaves, waxed paper, an iron.

What to do
Place a leaf between two pieces of waxed paper. Press it with a warm iron. Display it on a window, where light can shine through the 'sandwich'.

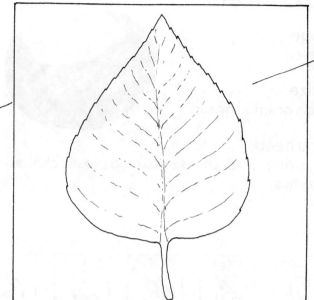

two sheets of waxed paper

leaf sandwiched between paper

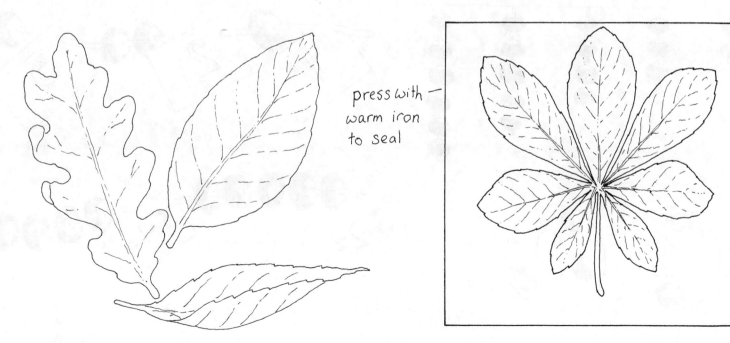

press with warm iron to seal

Using conkers

Age range
Five to seven.

Group size
Individuals or small group.

What you need
Conkers, string, card, cheese boxes, a plastic clothes-line, paint, brushes.

What to do
1 Use conkers hung on string and suspended from number cards to act as permanent number indicators.
2 Number cheese boxes and let the children place the corresponding number of conkers in each.
3 Thread groups of conkers on to a plastic clothes-line, interspersed with number cards.
4 Use unpainted conkers and red-painted conkers. Give children cards with simple addition sums written on them. The children then thread the corresponding numbers of different-coloured conkers on to a clothes-line and intersperse them with the addition cards, writing in the total on each card.

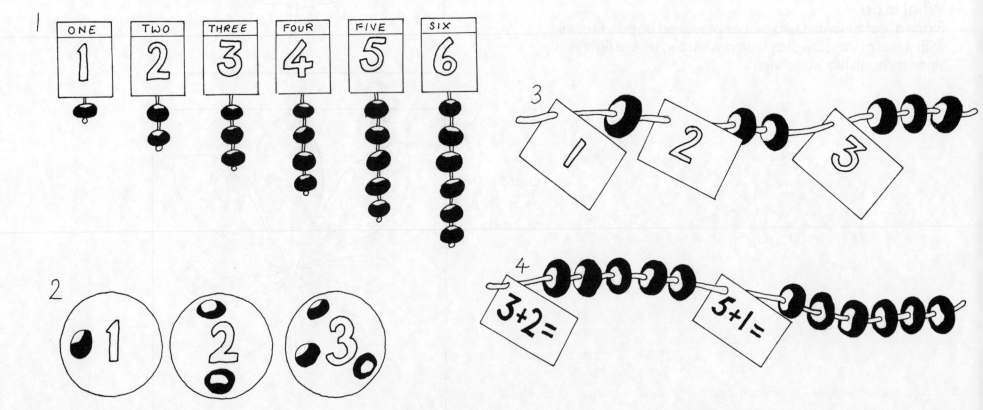

More conkers

Age range
Five to seven.

Group size
Whole class, then small groups.

What you need
Plenty of conkers (acorns would do just as well), a balance, writing materials.

What to do
Use the conkers as weights. Balance a variety of classroom objects against them and record the results, eg two conkers balance six pencils, five small conkers balance three larger ones.

Set the children oral or written tasks, eg find four conkers. Now find something which is a bit heavier/lighter/about the same weight as these.

Follow-up
Guess and then find out how many conkers fill a tin/box/jar. Half-fill a jug with water, then carefully put in enough conkers to make the water rise to fill the jug. How many conkers did you use? Try less or more water. Now how many conkers are needed? What would happen if you had a larger or smaller jug?

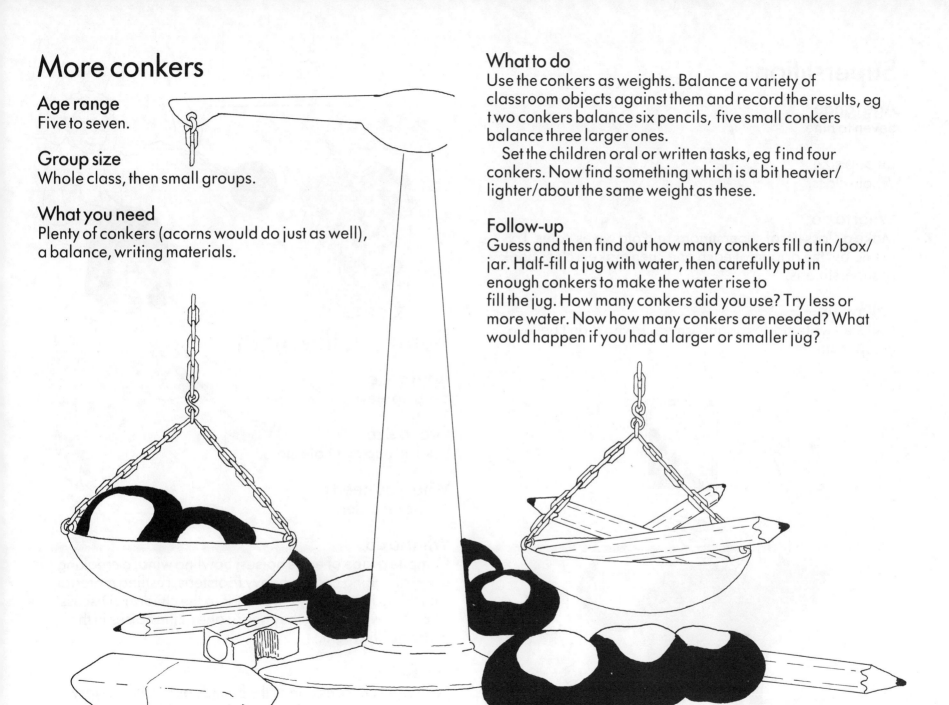

Superstitions

Age range
Seven to nine.

Group size
Whole class.

What to do
Make a class list of superstitions and old wives' tales. Try to find out the origins of each one, then make a class book of superstitions.

Follow-up
Children write stories about someone who didn't believe in superstitions.

Bumps in the night

Age range
Seven to eleven.

Group size
Small group or whole class.

What you need
A tape recorder.

What to do
Compile a tape of eerie noises: howling wind, a creaking door, dragging chains, heavy footsteps, rustling material, a cackling laugh. Play the sounds to the children. Discuss what they would do if they heard one of the noises in the middle of the night.

Follow-up
Each child chooses one of the sounds and writes a story about what happened when he/she went to investigate it.

Favourite horrors

Age range
Seven to nine.

Group size
Whole class.

What to do
Discuss unpleasant animals: spiders, snakes, bats, worms, etc. Make a graph showing children's favourite horrors in the insect and animal world.

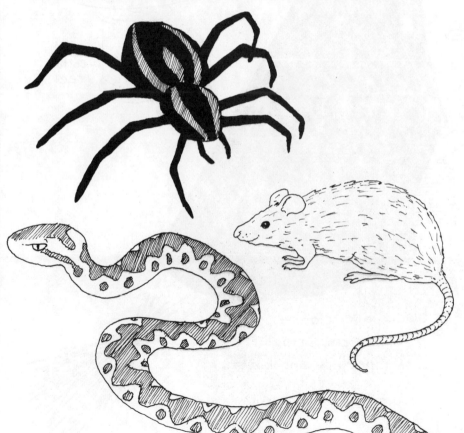

Witchy writing

Age range
Five to nine.

Group size
Individuals.

What to do
The children write or tell one of the following.

A story about what happens when a witch falls off her broomstick.

A description of a witch's face from a picture.

A list of all the things in an imaginary witch's cave.

A story about a witch who has an apple tree in her garden. Each year the tree bears just one apple – a magic one. What happens to the person who eats this special apple?

Flying witch

Age range
Five to eleven.

Group size
Individuals.

What you need
Cotton reels, wool, black paper, sticky tape, paper-fasteners, glue, straws, twigs, scissors.

What to do
Construct the witch as shown in the illustration and hang her from the ceiling as a mobile.

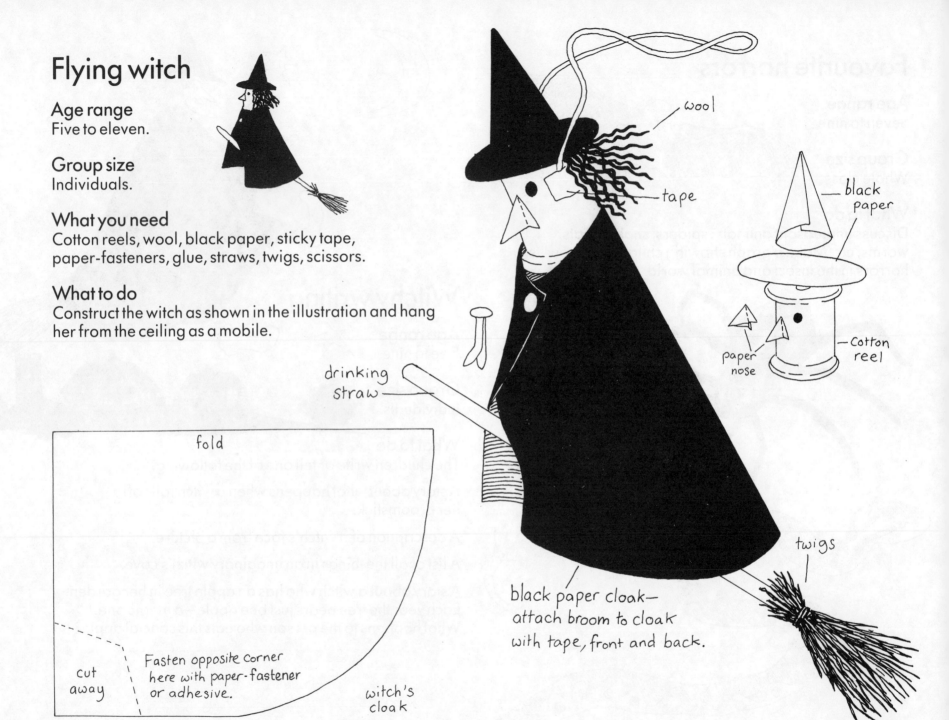

wool

tape

black paper

paper nose

Cotton reel

drinking straw

fold

cut away

Fasten opposite corner here with paper-fastener or adhesive.

witch's cloak

black paper cloak— attach broom to cloak with tape, front and back.

twigs

The witch game

Age range
Five to seven.

Group size
Whole class.

What to do
One child is the witch and thinks of a simple rule by which children can be chosen to go into her cooking pot – all those wearing something red, all the boys, all those with blue eyes, etc.

The children sit in a circle, with the witch in the middle. The witch chants:

'Bubble, bubble, boil and trouble,
The next one into the pot is . . .'

Then she pounces, picking someone who complies with her rule. The first child to realize what the rule is and shout it out becomes the next witch.

Follow-up
As a variation, give each child in the circle a logic block. The witch must then make her rule apply to, for example, all those children holding a blue shape, a triangle, a large shape, etc.

Hallowe'en masks

Age range
Seven to nine.

Group size
Individuals.

What you need
Card, scissors, raffia, crêpe paper, wool, paper, cotton wool, paints, brushes, foil, glue, pipe-cleaners, milk-bottle tops, material, thin elastic.

What to do
A witch mask is made from a pointed rectangle, monster and cat masks from circles. Cut the shapes from card, mark and cut out holes for eyes. Decorate the masks as shown and finish them off with thin elastic. When the children are wearing them, they could chant the spells they made up for the spell display on page 87.

Follow-up
Before letting the children take the masks home, use them as inspiration for dance, drama and creative writing.

hat: cut a cone of black paper and fringe the bottom - cut a brim to size, slip over the cone and secure to fringe.

foil moon

hair and eyebrows made from black raffia, strips of black crêpe paper or strands of wool

paper nose padded with cotton wool before sticking in place

Cut a ragged mouth with a few white card teeth and black gaps in between

face painted greyish-pink

warts: black tissue paper crumpled into balls

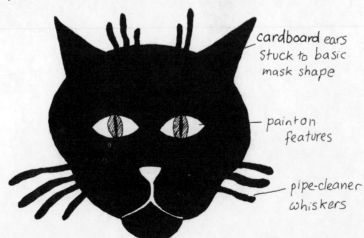

cardboard ears stuck to basic mask shape

paint on features

pipe-cleaner whiskers

wood shavings, wool, scraps of material, etc, to give a 'fantastic' appearance

cut a ragged shape around the edge of the mask

Spell display

Age range
Seven to nine.

Group size
Individuals.

What you need
Black sugar paper, white or coloured paper, scissors, glue, writing materials.

What to do
The witches' scene from *Macbeth* (Act IV Scene 1) is a good starter for this activity. Read the scene, then ask the children to make up their own recipes, including as many 'nasties' as they like. Write out the finished spells on white or coloured paper cut in toad, bat, snail or ghost shapes and display them on a large, black sugar-paper cauldron.

Follow-up
Act out your own witches' scene, using some of the children's spells in the dialogue.

Look up the dictionary definition of witch. Read it to the children and discuss it.

head of bee
wing of fly
hubble, bubble
junk yard
rubble

spiders leg
witch's hat
heat them up
and that
is that!

in our pot
there must go
leg of lamb
and green
frog's toe

Small shapes cut from white paper

black sugar-paper cauldron

Cats

Age range
Five to nine.

Group size
Whole class, then small groups.

What you need
Large sheets of paper (for juniors, some graph paper), writing materials.

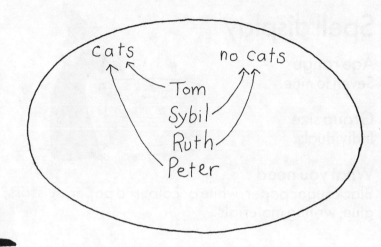

What to do
Discuss witches' cats (always black), then find out who in the class has/has not a cat. For juniors, this could be extended to several classes. Display the information as a simple mapping diagram.

Discuss the numbers involved, eg How many more children have a cat than haven't?

Follow-up
Transfer the mapping to a block graph, then an inclusion chart.

Practise sums with the numbers involved, eg In our class 15 children have cats. How can we make 15?

5+5+5

10+5

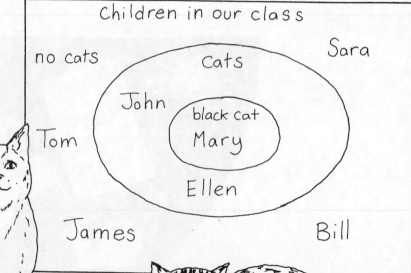

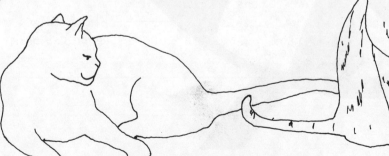

88

Costing cats

Age range
Seven to eleven.

Group size
Whole class or small group.

What you need
Sample tins of cat food or labels from tins; writing materials.

What to do
Work out the cost of feeding a cat for a week. Compare the prices of different brands of cat food and work out the most/least expensive.

Follow-up
Record the information on a graph and display this with cat-food labels.

   Work out how much the average cat costs to keep during its lifetime. What else would that money buy? Ask cat owners to try to justify spending such a sum of money on their cat. Do the same for other pet animals.

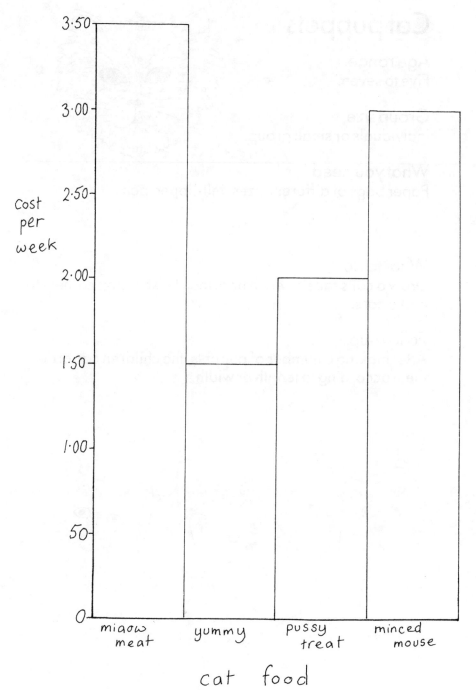

89

Cat puppets

Age range
Five to seven.

Group size
Individuals or small group.

What you need
Paper bags of different sizes, felt-tipped pens.

What to do
Draw a cat's face on each bag, then twist the top corners to make ears.

Follow-up
After making a number of puppets, the children can order them according to length or width.

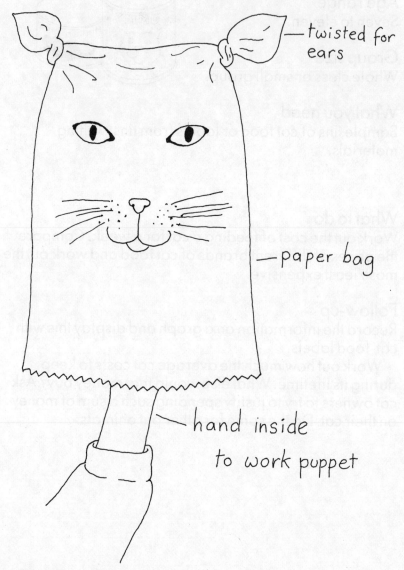

twisted for ears

paper bag

hand inside to work puppet

Cat sorting cards

Age range
Five to seven.

Group size
Individuals.

What you need
Card, writing materials.

What to do
Make two sets of cards with 12 to 20 cards in each set. The first set should show cats of the same shape, but of different sizes and with tails of different lengths. The biggest cat should not have the longest tail, nor the smallest cat the shortest.

The second set should show cats of the same size, but with differences in appearance: with or without tails or whiskers, with tails curled in different directions, etc. Make some of the cats identical.

Children order the first set of cards according to the cats' lengths, widths or tail lengths.

The second set can be used to play snap, to sort according to different criteria and to practise addition by joining both sets of cats and counting the total.

Follow-up
Worksheets can be made to use with the cards.

Sample cards from set 1

Put the cats in order.
Trace the third cat.
Colour it blue.

work card for use with set 1

sample cards from set 2

91

What is fog?

Age range
Seven to nine.

Group size
Small group.

What you need
Paper plates, scissors, cotton wool or fine gauze, sticky tape, string.

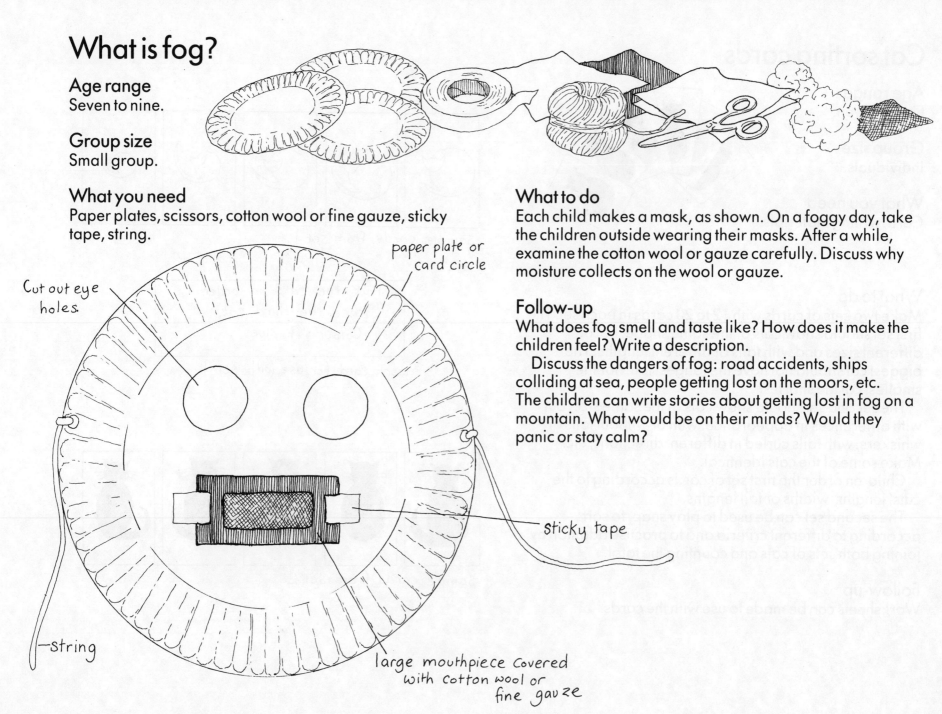

Cut out eye holes.

paper plate or card circle

sticky tape

string

large mouthpiece covered with cotton wool or fine gauze

What to do
Each child makes a mask, as shown. On a foggy day, take the children outside wearing their masks. After a while, examine the cotton wool or gauze carefully. Discuss why moisture collects on the wool or gauze.

Follow-up
What does fog smell and taste like? How does it make the children feel? Write a description.
   Discuss the dangers of fog: road accidents, ships colliding at sea, people getting lost on the moors, etc. The children can write stories about getting lost in fog on a mountain. What would be on their minds? Would they panic or stay calm?

Chocolate fudge

Age range
Seven to eleven.

Group size
Small group.

What you need
450 g granulated sugar
150 ml evaporated milk
150 ml water
25 g cocoa
50 g margarine
3 drops vanilla essence

What to do
Put all the ingredients except the essence into a large saucepan. Heat them gently until the fat is melted and the sugar has dissolved. Boil the mixture for 5 minutes, stirring it all the time. Put a drop of the mixture into a saucer of cold water; if it forms a soft ball, remove the saucepan from the heat. Beat the mixture until it is thick and creamy. Pour it into a greased tin and leave it to cool. Before the fudge is set, mark it into squares with a knife.

Place all ingredients — apart from essence in the saucepan.

To test when mixture is ready — put a drop into a saucer of cold water.

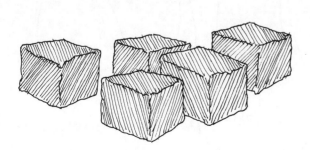

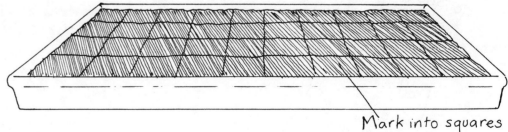

Mark into squares before fudge sets.

Firework-night party

Age range
Nine to eleven.

Group size
Whole class or small group.

What to do
In groups of four to six, draw up a list of children invited to the firework party. Discuss the food needed. Cost the total food to be bought, then find the cost per head. Costs may be known already, found on packets or the information may be brought in from home. It may not be possible to have such a party at school, but it can be planned nevertheless.

Follow-up
Set the children problems such as this one: if everyone at the party shakes hands once with everyone else, how many handshakes would there be? (Imagine there were only two people, three people, four, etc.) Can this be illustrated? Can you think of a way of recording this?

Fire words

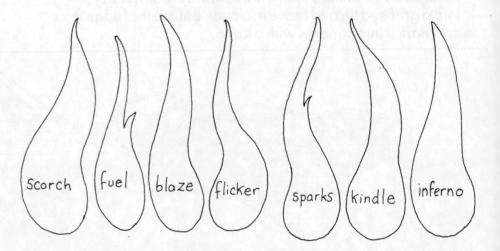

Age range
Seven to nine.

Group size
Whole class.

What you need
Orange, red and yellow sugar paper, pens.

What to do
Make a class list of fire words – all the words which describe the sight, smell, colours, shapes or movements of fire. Write the words on flame-shaped pieces of orange, yellow or red paper and display them as a growing bonfire.

Follow-up
Extend the list to include compound words which have 'fire' at the beginning or end: fire alarm, firefly, bonfire, campfire, etc.

Flame movement sequence

Age range
Seven to eleven.

Group size
Whole class.

What to do
Discuss and list words which describe how flames move:
flicker, leap, sink, writhe, twist, spurt, dwindle, jump, curl.
Each child then chooses a word and moves accordingly
(eg flicker – short, sharp jerky movements), saying the
word softly over and over as they do so. After the children
have each tried out several words, build up a flame
sequence.

Follow-up
Extend by dividing the class into two groups: flames and
bonfire builders. Each builder leads a flame to the fire,
arranging it as they wish. The builders then mime lighting
the fire and the flames move through the sequences they
have practised, while the builders dance round them. As
the flames die down, the builders rest on the floor.

For added effect, the flames can carry red or orange
scarves and the builders can play percussion instruments
as they dance.

WINTER

Displays and collections

Warm winter clothes
Hot-water bottles, warming pans and bed socks
Buds
Candles and candlesticks
Lamps
Umbrellas
Heart-shaped things
Boots and winter shoes
Gloves and mittens
Winter foods
Waterproof materials
Calendars
Shiny and dull things
White and silver things
Frying pans
Winter sports equipment
Bells

Topic work

Winter sports
Stars
Gifts and giving
Birthdays
Ice, snow and frost
Cold
Rain
Birds
Light
Friendship
Time
Parties
Buds
Forms of heating
Insulation

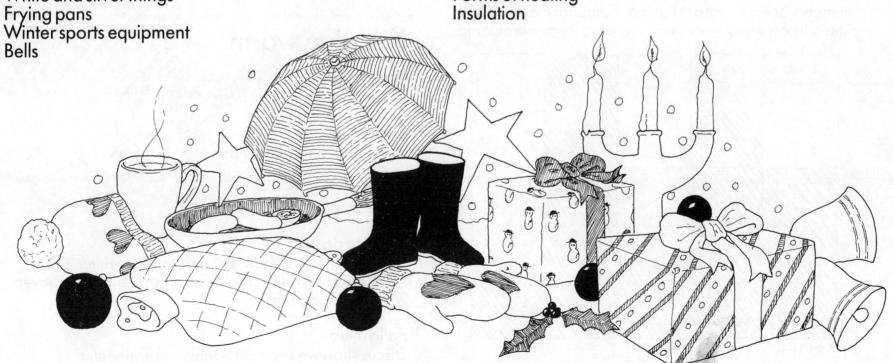

Wet-weather clothes

Age range
Five to seven.

Group size
Small group.

What to do
Children make a class survey of the wet-weather clothes worn to school. Working in pairs, they find out who wore boots/macs/anoraks/capes and who had an umbrella (one pair should be responsible for each item).

Follow-up
Use the information to make a bar chart showing the numbers of each item of clothing. Compare the totals to find out how many more macs there are than anoraks, etc.

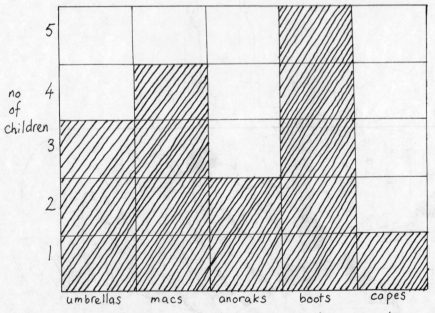

There are two more macs than anoraks.
Five children wore boots.

We wear warm hats.

We put hot water bottles in our beds.

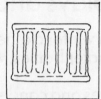

We turn on radiators.

We have hot drinks.

We wear gloves.

We put on warm coats.

Keeping warm

Age range
Five to seven.

Group size
Individuals and whole class.

What you need
Paints, paper.

What to do
Make a class list of how we keep warm in winter. Each child illustrates one of the ideas; these are then displayed with simple captions.

Follow-up
Discuss how we keep our homes warm in winter.

Winter figure

Age range
Five to seven.

Group size
Whole class.

What you need
Scraps of fabric, glue, scissors, a large sheet of paper, a pen.

What to do
One member of the class puts on his/her outdoor clothes. Make a list of these and add any other warm clothes the children can think of.

Draw round another child, cut out the outline and dress it in winter clothes using scraps of fabric. Label the figure with appropriate vocabulary.

Follow-up
Do the same with summer clothes, or rainy-day clothes.

what do we wear in winter?

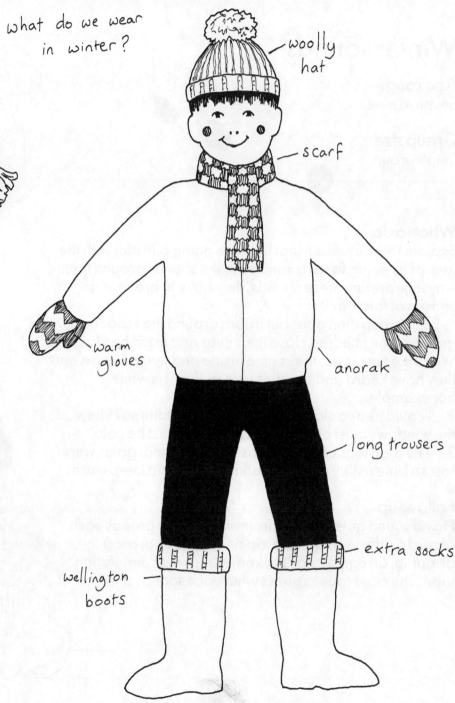

woolly hat

scarf

warm gloves

anorak

long trousers

extra socks

wellington boots

Winter sounds

Age range
Seven to nine.

Group size
Small group.

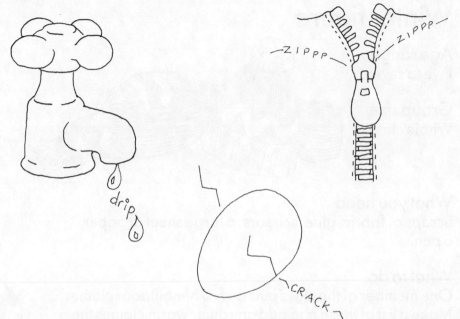

What to do
Explain to the children that they are going outside, with the task of listening for two minutes to the sounds around them – by interpreting these sounds, they have to prove what season of the year it is.

Each group then goes out in turn around the school grounds, the children close their eyes and listen hard. When the time is up, they come inside and write down what they have heard and how this proves that it is winter. For example:

1   I could hear a class singing, but it was faint so I knew the windows must be closed, so I knew it must be cold.
2   The footsteps of people passing the school gates were fast so I knew they must be walking quickly to keep warm.

Follow-up
Play a sound guessing game. Individuals or groups each record a different sound (a zip being done up, a tap dripping, an egg being cracked) to make a compilation tape. The class tries to guess what each sound is.

Ladybird, ladybird

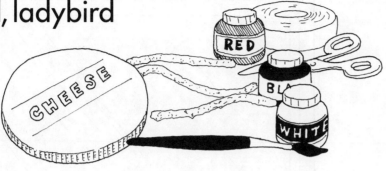

Age range
Five to seven.

Group size
Individuals.

What you need
Round cheese boxes, pipe-cleaners, card, black, white and red paint, brushes, scissors, sticky tape.

What to do
For each ladybird, take half a cheese box, paint it red and allow it to dry. Cut the pipe-cleaners into lengths, six long lengths for the legs and two shorter lengths for the antennae. Cut three slits in each side of the cheese box and insert a leg into each, bending them to form a curved shape. Attach the antennae to a cardboard circle and fix them to one end of the cheese box with sticky tape. Mark on the ladybird's spots and paint the legs and antennae black.

Follow-up
Pin the ladybirds to the wall, so that they appear to be crawling along it.

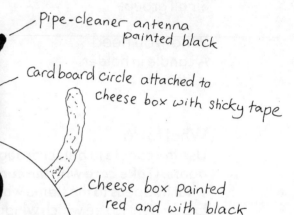

Pipe-cleaner antenna painted black

Cardboard circle attached to cheese box with sticky tape

Cheese box painted red and with black spots

pipe-cleaner legs painted black

Draught detector

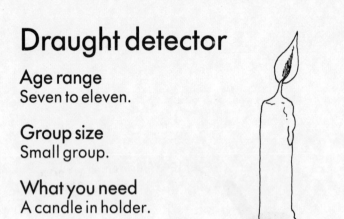

Age range
Seven to eleven.

Group size
Small group.

What you need
A candle in holder.

What to do
Use the candle to detect draughts near windows and doors. (**Take care with the candles, of course.**) Watch what happens to the flame when a door is opened. Experiment to see which window must be opened to make the flame bend in a certain direction. Does the flame point in the same direction near the top of a partly-opened door as it does near the bottom?

Follow-up
The children record their experiments and findings. Discuss methods of draught-proofing windows and doors.

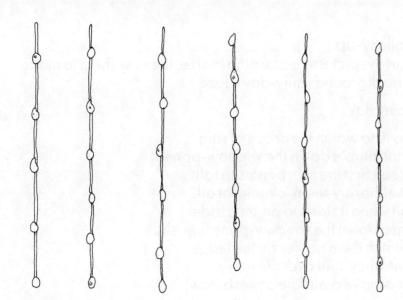

Artificial rain

Age range
Five to nine.

Group size
Small group.

What you need
Strands of cotton, PVA glue.

What to do
Place several strands of cotton on a Formica-topped table and put blobs of the glue at intervals down the length of each strand. Leave them overnight, then carefully peel the strands of cotton off the table. Hang the strands from the ceiling to make a shower of rain.

Follow-up
Suspend several lengths of rain in front of a frieze to make a rainy-day scene, or in front of a rainy-word bank.

Weather checks

Age range
Seven to nine.

Group size
Small group.

What to do
It is often said that cold weather kills germs. The children can test the truth of this saying by making a survey of the number of children absent from school each day and relating this to a record of weather conditions. (Don't name the children, simply record the number absent.)

Another weather saying is, 'As the days lengthen, the cold begins to strengthen'. Take temperature readings for the weeks before and after the shortest day. Is the weather really colder after the shortest day than it was before?

Follow-up
Make graphs of the results and display these with written work.

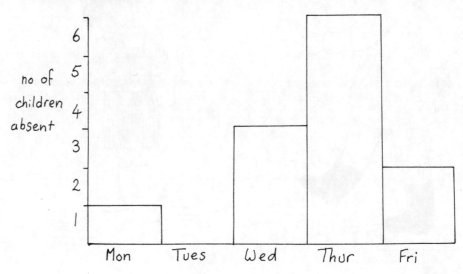

Rainy day

Age range
Five to seven.

Group size
Small group or whole class.

What you need
Crayons or paints, paper, scissors.

What to do
Talk about rainy-day clothes. The children draw themselves dressed for wet weather, colour or paint the pictures and cut them out.

Follow-up
Sort the pictures according to size, then use them to make a background rainy-day frieze.

Rainy day

I love to watch the drops of rain
That tumble down the window-pane.
When first the rain begins to fall
They hardly seem to move at all.
But when it starts to pour outside,
Then down the window-pane they slide.
I watch them gather on the ledge
Until they spill over the edge
And make a puddle down below:
I see it grow . . . and grow . . . and grow.
Then when the shower of rain has passed,
And I'm allowed outside at last,
In big strong boots I go to see
The paddling place that's all for me!

Red sky at night

Age range
Seven to eleven.

Group size
Small group or whole class.

What to do
Make a list of country sayings about weather.

The longer the day, the fiercer the cold.

Red sky at night is shepherd's delight.

Red sky in the morning is shepherd's warning.

One swallow does not make a summer.

A wet March makes a sad harvest.

A green Christmas makes a full churchyard.

The children then try to make up some of their own rhymes, serious or humorous.

Follow-up
Discuss the origins of weather sayings. Why did people need to make them up?

105

Shapely decorations

Age range
Five to seven.

Group size
Whole class, then small group.

What you need
Junk boxes, tins or cartons, some coloured paper, drawing materials, glue.

What to do
Each child chooses a tin, box, or carton. Discuss the shapes at the top and bottom of the various containers. Are they the same shape and size? Have they straight sides or curved? The children then draw round the tops and bottoms on to coloured paper and cut out the shapes. Before sticking them down, sort the shapes in different ways and discuss simple properties, eg the number of sides and corners.

Follow-up
Use the shapes to form festive figures and record them. Use the shapes to decorate paper table-cloths (see 'Party table-cloths' on page 107), calendars, windows, gifts, wrapping paper, etc.

I used two circles one triangle and four rectangles for my clown.

I used five triangles two circles and two rectangles for my king.

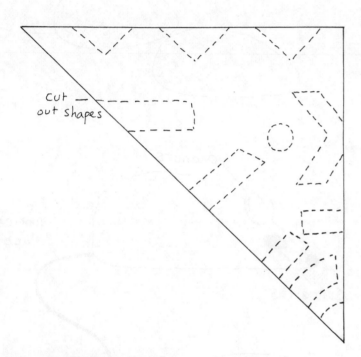

Party table-cloths

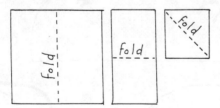

Age range
Five to nine.

Group size
Small group.

What you need
Large pieces of white and brightly-coloured paper, scissors, newspaper, paints.

What to do
Cut a large piece of white paper to the size of the required table-cloth. Fold it in half, in half again, then diagonally. Cut shapes along the fold. Unfold the paper and stick it to a similarly-sized, brightly-coloured piece of paper.

Alternatively, use newspaper for folding and cutting, fix it to background paper, and use it as a stencil.

Sugar mice

Age range
Five to nine.

Group size
Small group.

What you need
1 egg white
450 g icing sugar (have an extra bag ready
    to help mould the mice)
Currants
Peanuts
Liquorice laces

What to do
Whisk the egg white until it is white and frothy. Add the
icing sugar and mix until a stiff, pliable paste is formed.
Divide the mixture into 12 small balls. Mould each ball into
a mouse shape. Add currants for nose and eyes, peanuts
for ears and liquorice laces for tails.

Follow-up
Before taking them home or eating them, use the mice for
some number work: estimate, then check, each mouse's
weight, order them by weight, measure the length of each
mouse's tail.
    Make small mouse-shaped books, containing the
recipe, tail lengths and weights of the mice.

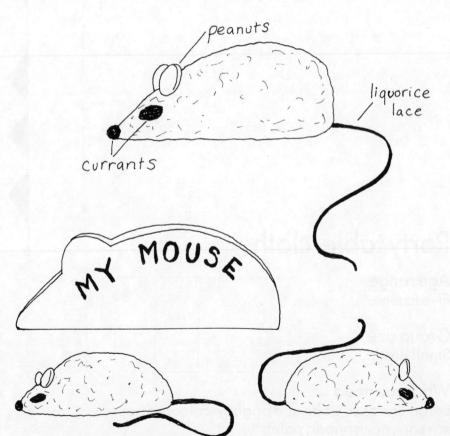

peanuts

liquorice
lace

currants

MY MOUSE

Party-hat game

Age range
Five to seven.

Group size
Whole class.

What you need
Party hats.

What to do
Five children stand in a row, each wearing a different party hat. While the rest of the children close their eyes, two of the children in the row change hats. The children open their eyes and say whose hats have changed.

Theatre calendar

Age range
Nine to eleven.

Group size
Individuals.

What you need
For each calendar you need a box approximately 16×11×13 cm, scissors, 12 pieces of thin card 4 cm taller than the box and 3 cm less than its width, crayons, a calendar tab, glue.

month page from calendar tab

cut decorative design in top of each card

appropriate design for each month

month cards — make 12

month cards slotted in to box

What to do
Cut a rectangular hole in the front of the box, leaving about 4 cm at the sides and 2 cm at the top and bottom. Cut decorative designs along the tops of the pieces of card (cut one, then use it as a template for the others). Cut a slot in the top of the box wide enough and deep enough to take all 12 cards. Decorate each card with a design appropriate to a different month and add the relevant page from the calendar tab to the top. Decorate the outside of the box, then slot the cards in the top.

Put the card for the present month to the front, so that the calendar tab shows above the box and the design on the card can be seen through the hole in the front of the box.

Follow-up
Change the card each month.

Perpetual calendar

Age range
Nine to eleven.

Group size
Individuals or small group.

What you need
Thick card, scissors, paper-fasteners, writing materials.

What to do
To make each calendar, cut out two similarly-sized circles from paper and mark them up as shown. Paste them to card circles. Cut out two pointers from the card. Assemble the discs and pointers in the following order, top to bottom: day pointer, upper disc, date pointer, bottom disc. Put a paper-fastener through holes in the centre of each disc and pointer to secure them.

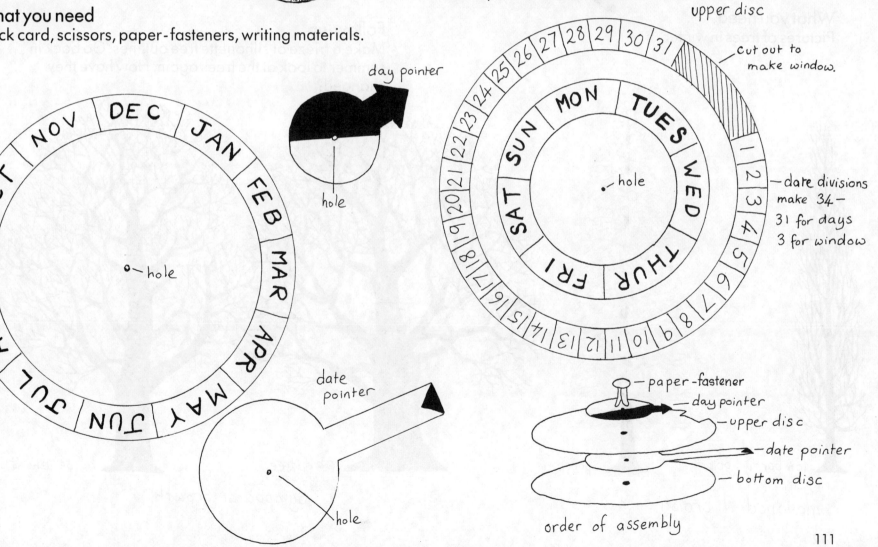

bottom disc

day pointer

hole

date pointer

hole

upper disc

cut out to make window.

hole

date divisions make 34 —
31 for days
3 for window

paper-fastener

day pointer

upper disc

date pointer

bottom disc

order of assembly

111

Winter trees

Age range
Seven to nine.

Group size
Small group or whole class.

What you need
Pictures of trees in winter.

What to do
Take the children out to look at tree outlines or show them pictures of various species. Can they identify the tree from the shape of its outline? Look carefully at the way the branches are arranged and classify the trees according to whether growth takes place from the terminal bud (monopodial growth) or from the side buds (sympodial growth).

Follow-up
Make a frieze of silhouette tree outlines. Go back in summer to look at the trees again. How have they changed?

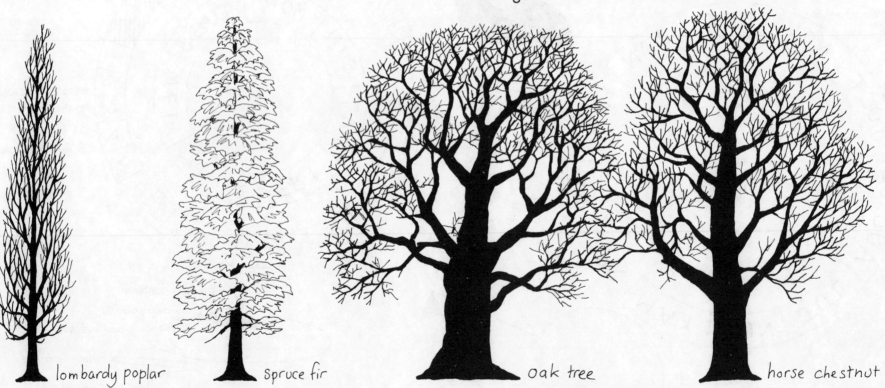

lombardy poplar   spruce fir   oak tree   horse chestnut

monopodial growth   Sympodial growth

Ice-cube competition

Age range
Nine to eleven.

Group size
Small group.

What you need
Ice cubes.

What to do
The children hold a competition to see who can melt their ice cubes first, without using artificial heat or crushing the ice (hint – rub your hands before clasping the ice cube).

Follow-up
Repeat the competition, but this time see who can keep their cubes from melting for the longest time (try wrapping cubes in cotton wool, foil, newspaper, or putting them in a thermos flask).

Tracks

Age range
Five to seven.

Group size
Small group.

Mount each print on a piece of card—children can then sort the footprints into pairs

boot prints—paint soles and press on paper

wash thoroughly afterwards!

What to do
On a snowy day, take groups of children outside to look for tracks. Begin by looking at the tracks made by the children's own boots or shoes. Can they identify which footprints are from which shoe or boot by the pattern of the soles? How can they tell a left footprint from a right one?

Look for other footprints. Can they find some made by a man, a woman and a child? How do they differ? Are there any tyre tracks? What kind of vehicle made them?

Now try to find some animal or bird tracks. Can the children tell where the animal was going? Was the bird hopping or walking?

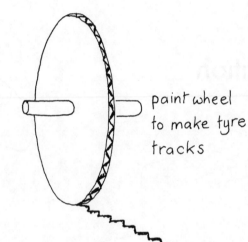

paint wheel to make tyre tracks

drawn or printed shapes (use potatoes)

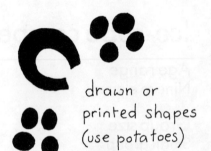

Follow-up
Children can record the tracks they have seen by drawing them on white paper, printing them with boots, or using paint wheels or modelling clay.

bird walking

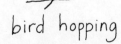

bird hopping

Snowstorms

Age range
Seven to nine.

Group size
Individuals.

What you need
Glue, screw-top jars, Christmas-cake decorations, desiccated coconut.

What to do
Glue a Christmas-cake decoration inside the screw-top lid of a jar. Fill the jar with water and add a sprinkling of desiccated coconut. Screw the lid tightly to the jar. Turn the jar upside-down and shake it to see the snow fall.

jar filled with water and dessicated coconut

Christmas-cake decoration

screw-top lid

115

Winter sports

Age range
Nine to eleven.

Group size
Small group.

What to do
The children research and compile descriptions of various winter sports. They should also list the equipment used for each sport and mention any rules or scoring methods. The sports include those in which the children may have participated — tobogganing, making snowmen, sliding or snowballing — and more unusual ones, such as skating, skiing, curling, ski-jumping and skate racing.

Follow-up
Make a collection of equipment (skates, sledge, etc) and display it on a table in front of a large winter-scene collage. Display the writing around the collage.

Skating:
You need —
skates

Skiing:
You need —
skis, goggles, boots, poles

Snow balling:
You need —
snow

Snowman building:
You need —
snow, hat, coal, scarf, carrot, twig

tobogganing:
you need —
toboggan

Snowman sorting cards

Age range
Five to seven.

Group size
Individuals or pairs.

What you need
Card, felt-tipped pens.

What to do
Make 20 or 30 cards, each showing a snowman of the same shape and size, but with slight variations: with/without scarf, with three/four buttons, with a red/black hat, etc. Make some snowmen exactly the same so that snap can be played. Children can also sort the cards in different ways, explaining the criteria they have used each time.

Away, Jack Frost!

Age range
Five to seven.

Group size
Large group or whole class.

What to do
One child, Jack Frost, is in the centre of a ring of children.
Another child, Spring, is waiting outside the ring.

Jack Frost: I'll nip your fingers,
                 I'll nip your toes,
                 I'll nip your ears,
                 And nip your nose.

Children: We'll move our fingers,
                 We'll wriggle our toes,
                 We'll rub our ears,
                 And we'll nip your nose!

Jack Frost: I'll freeze the water
On the ground,
I'll burst your pipes
Without a sound.

Spring: Yes, Jack Frost,
The children know
You've lost your sting —
So away you go!

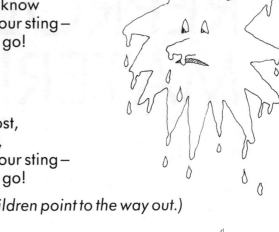

Children: You can freeze the water —
Then we'll skate,
And we'll send for the plumber
Before it's too late!

Children: Yes, Jack Frost,
We all know,
You've lost your sting —
So away you go!

(Jack Frost hurries out. Children point to the way out.)

Jack Frost: Oh, dearie me,
I'm losing my sting,
Why! No wonder!
Here comes Spring!

(Children allow Spring to enter the ring.)

REPRODUCIBLE
MATERIAL

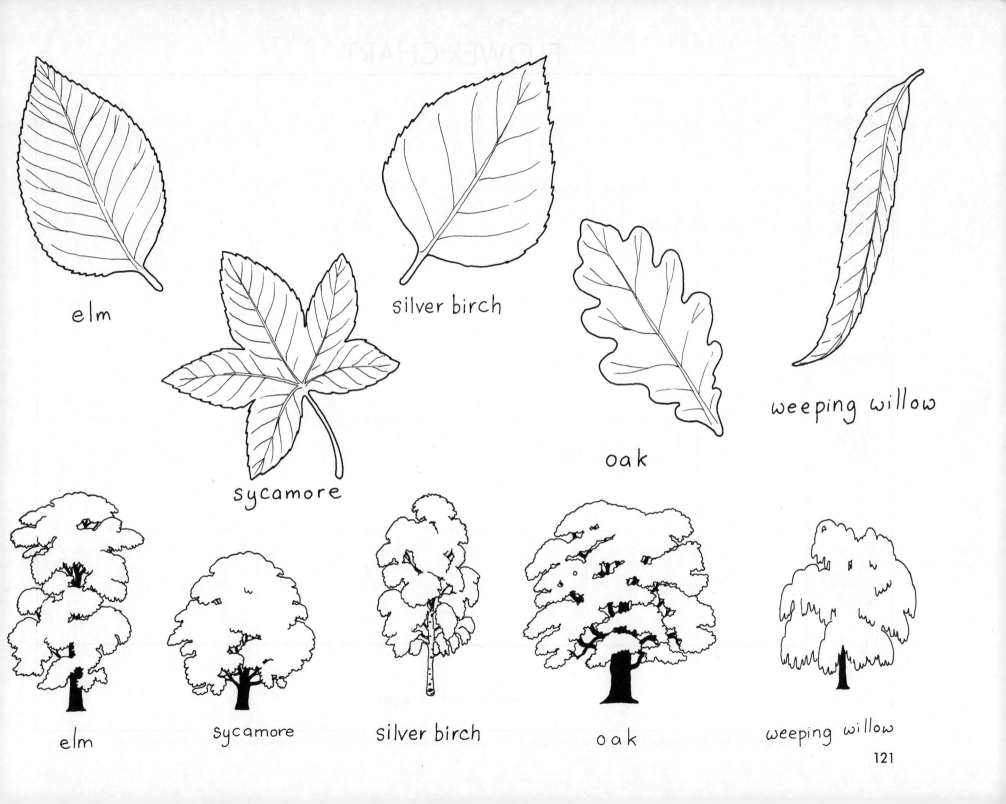

elm

sycamore

silver birch

oak

weeping willow

elm

sycamore

silver birch

oak

weeping willow

FLOWER CHART

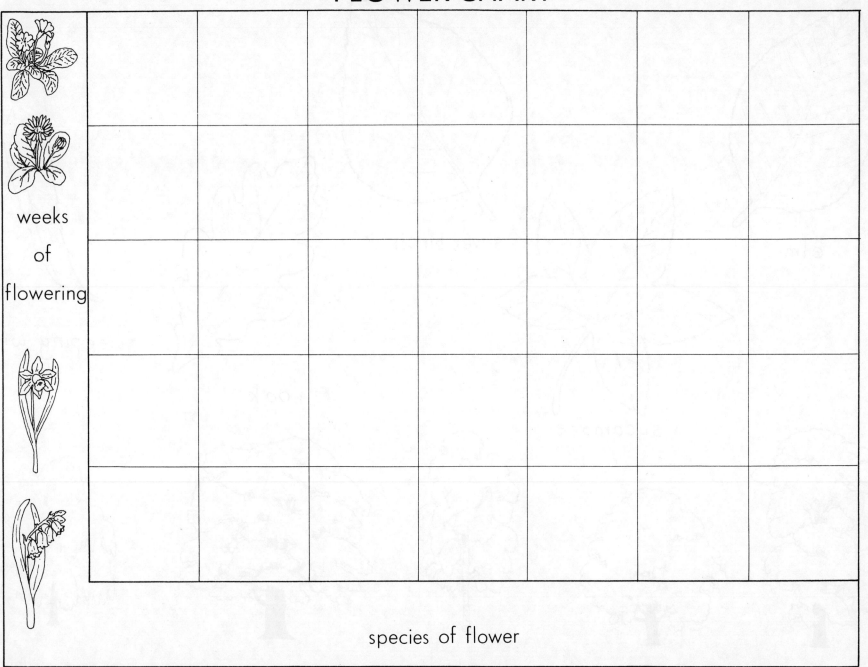

weeks

of

flowering

species of flower

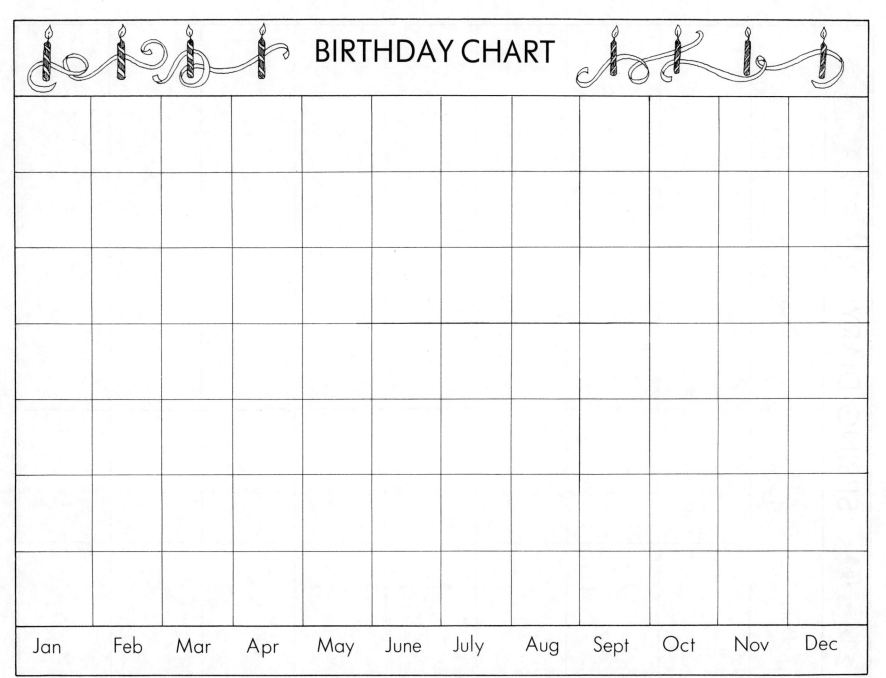

BIRTHDAY CHART

Jan	Feb	Mar	Apr	May	June	July	Aug	Sept	Oct	Nov	Dec

SPRING DIARY

Date	Today I saw	Drawing

SUMMER DIARY

Date	Today I saw	Drawing

AUTUMN DIARY

Date	Today I saw	Drawing

WINTER DIARY

Date	Today I saw	Drawing

ACKNOWLEDGEMENTS

The editors and publisher extend grateful thanks for the reuse of material first published in *Child Education* to: Kate Stewart for 'All sorts of weather'; Eunice Close for 'Mad March wind' and 'Windy day'; Ivy Russell for 'Rainy day'; Marguerite Turnbull for 'Sky picture'; Jean Root for 'Apples, apples, one, two, three'; W O'Neill for 'Away Jack Frost!'

Every effort has been made to trace and acknowledge contributors. If any right has been omitted, the publishers offer their apologies and will rectify this in subsequent editions following notification.

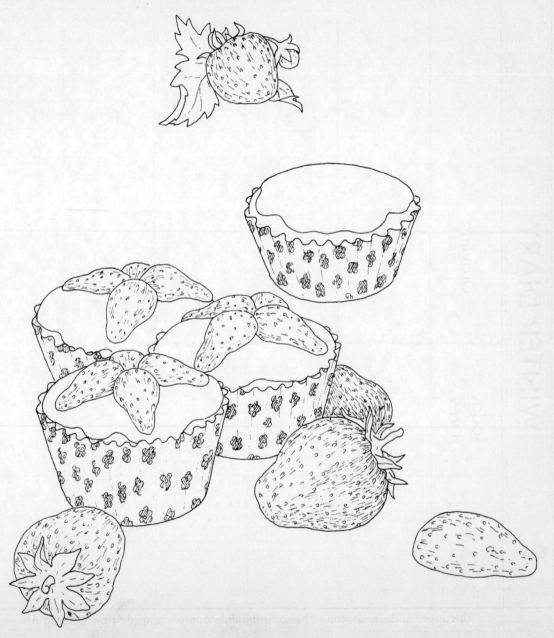